Cowboys and Coffin Makers

One Hundred 19th-Century Jobs You Might Have Feared or Fancied

by Laurie Coulter
art by Martha Newbigging

annick press
toronto + new york + vancouver

We acknowledge the support of the Canada Council for the Arts, the Ontario Arts Council, and the Government of Canada through the Book Publishing Industry Development Program (BPIDP) for our publishing activities.

Cataloging in Publication

Coulter, Laurie, 1951-
    Cowboys and coffin makers : one hundred 19th-century jobs you might have feared or fancied / by Laurie Coulter ; illustrated by Martha Newbigging.

Includes index.
ISBN-13: 978-1-55451-068-9 (bound)
ISBN-10: 1-55451-068-6 (bound)
ISBN-13: 978-1-55451-067-2 (pbk.)
ISBN-10: 1-55451-067-8 (pbk.)

    1. Occupations—United States—History—19th century—Juvenile literature. I. Newbigging, Martha II. Title.

HD8072.C69 2007   j331.700973'09034   C2006-905789-3

Distributed in Canada by:
Firefly Books Ltd.
66 Leek Crescent
Richmond Hill, ON
L4B 1H1

Published in the U.S.A. by Annick Press (U.S.) Ltd.
Distributed in the U.S.A. by:
Firefly Books (U.S.) Inc.
P.O. Box 1338
Ellicott Station
Buffalo, NY 1420

Printed in China.

Visit us at: www.annickpress.com

Contents

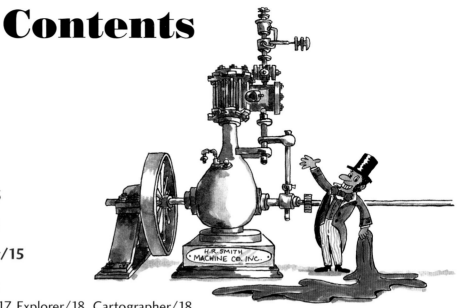

Introduction

This book is about the great changes that took place in 19th-century America and how those changes affected people's jobs in good or nasty ways. It looks at ordinary lives rather than famous people and events, because entire books have been written on one person, or one war, or one invention. If this book encourages you to read more on this incredible century, it will have done its job well.

The Industrial Revolution began in Britain in the 1700s. It made that small island country the most powerful trading nation in the world  during the reign of Queen Victoria, from 1837 to 190. (She's the reason people from that time are called Victorians.) Newly invented machines that ran on the energy of high-pressure steam sped up the mining of coal and the production of textiles, iron, and manufactured goods. The British flooded the world with their factory-made products.

For a time, Americans looked down their noses at the poorly paid men, women, and children slogging away in the horrible working conditions of Britain's factories. They were happy to be farmers, craftspeople, or merchants importing British goods. Gradually, though, British technical knowledge made its way across the Atlantic, and Americans began getting in on the act. Sometimes they put a new lever on this machine or a new wheel on that machine and came up with better machines. The American Industrial Revolution may have had a slow start, but the country caught up so quickly that by the end of the 19th century it

had overtaken Britain as the world's leading industrial nation.

You may have heard about *future shock*: it's being stressed out by rapid technological change. Well, Americans in the 1800s were one shocked bunch. For the most part, they adjusted well and found many of the changes exciting. People were amazed at how quickly they could cross the country on the new trains or zoom up a building in the new elevators. At first they weren't even sure it was safe to travel so fast or in such strange contraptions.

The many changes in this century didn't begin and end with machines. People were also bombarded with new scientific discoveries and new ideas about slavery, religion, politics, workers' rights, education, public health—the list goes on. Victorians may have been "future-shocked" by the Industrial Revolution, but they loved to talk and read about it, and to come up with even more ways to transform their world.

Horace Wifflehammer's Job

To get an idea of how one particular job changed from the beginning to the end of the century, let's take a peek at how office clerk Horace Wifflehammer spends his day. In the early 1800s, Horace walks to his job in a small building lit by oil lamps on gloomy days. He works with his uncle, who runs an import-export business that brings foreign manufactured goods into the country and sends American cotton, whale oil, fish, furs, and lumber overseas. While another clerk adds up figures in an account book, Horace writes letters with a quill pen. His uncle works beside him, training his nephew in the business.

By the end of the century, Horace rides an electric trolley to work from his home in the suburbs, takes an elevator up to his gaslit office, and works with dozens of other clerks for a large railroad company. He uses a machine to add up figures, writes with a fountain pen, telephones distant customers, and works alongside—gasp!—a woman. She taps out letters on a typewriter while a manager tells Horace what to do. He's never met the owner of the business.

Powerful Changes

English immigrant Samuel Slater builds a water-powered cotton-spinning mill in Rhode Island, the first modern factory in America. In the South, Eli Whitney invents the cotton gin, a machine that speeds up the production of cotton fiber to feed the new textile industry of the North.

The beginning of a very steamy century. Oliver Evans's high-pressure steam engine powers Robert Fulton's new steamboat and eventually railroad locomotives. Wood fires heat homes and boil water in boilers to produce the steam that drives the new engines. The United States begins to expand across the continent with the purchase of the Louisiana Territory from France. Population in 1800: about 5 million.

1790 **1800** **1810**

Boston merchant Francis Cabot Lowell returns from Britain with a mill in his brain. Britain prevents any machinery or drawings from leaving its shores, so Lowell memorizes how one of their complicated power looms works. When he arrives home, he builds a better one and founds the first water-powered mill to carry out spinning and weaving under one roof.

Connecticut inventor Eli Terry and his associates use water-powered machines to mass-produce wooden clocks. Instead of one skilled person making an entire clock by hand, several not-so-skilled people make uniform, interchangeable clock parts by machine. This faster manufacturing technique becomes known as the "American system."

The gaslight era begins. Underground pipes carry gas made from coal into city streetlamps and buildings. Work and entertainment expand into the evening hours.

On a good road, a team of four horses can haul 1½ tons of goods a day. On the new man-made waterways, or canals, the same team walking along a towpath beside the canal can pull a barge loaded with 100 tons and haul it six miles (almost 10 km) farther. Many immigrants digging canals.

Grub break!

The new railroad network needs a safer, faster traffic control system. Samuel F.B. Morse's electric telegraph system replaces flagmen. Telegraph operators can signal ahead on the progress of each train. The railroads run on time and telegraph wires soon carry messages about all sorts of things—deaths in the family, weather reports, and news. Coal begins to replace wood for heating homes and charcoal for fueling iron blast furnaces. Everybody digging during the gold rush in California.

1820

1830

1840

1850

Mills start using steam-powered machinery rather than water-powered machinery, which has to be shut down when rivers freeze during the winter. The Baltimore & Ohio Railroad begins running steam-powered trains along a 13-mile (21 km) stretch of track. Railroad and canal companies fight a bitter war for business, which is eventually won by the men with "iron horses" rather than the men with real horses pulling boats. Many immigrants digging railroad beds.

The first American oil well gushes 500 barrels a month in Pennsylvania. The oil is burned in lamps and used to lubricate machinery. (It won't be used as a fuel until late in the century.) The new sewing machine revolutionizes the manufacture of clothing.

The North and South fight a war over slavery, among other things, and the North wins. The transcontinental telegraph line and the transcontinental railroad are both completed. Most powerful change: African-American slaves are freed.

Thomas Edison builds a direct-current (DC) power plant and lights up some buildings in New York City. His rival, Nikola Tesla, invents alternating-current (AC) electricity. George Westinghouse buys the patent rights to Tesla's system and opens the world's first hydroelectric plant at Niagara Falls. Electric trolleys push aside cable cars.

| | 1860 | | 1880 | |
| | | 1870 | | 1890 |

A decade of big brains. Alexander Graham Bell invents the telephone and organizes the Bell Telephone Company. Thomas Edison opens his "invention factory," which turns out (among many other inventions) the phonograph, the motion picture projector, and the electric light bulb. Cable cars begin running on city streets. Many would-be farmers digging up sod on the Great Plains.

Giant corporations rule. Labor unions fight back. Charles Duryea builds the first gasoline-powered car, but it is automaker Henry Ford who is remembered today. The populations of cities and towns explode in the half-century after the Civil War. At the turn of the century, about 76 million Americans get around with 18 million horses and mules, 10 million bicycles, 30,000 electric trolleys, and 8,000 cars.

No Idle Hands

To not work in the 1800s was shameful. You were called a "lubber" or a "sluggard." In many families, everyone had to work to survive. In 1800, only a tiny number of Americans lived in towns of more than 8,000 people. Most lived on farms, where work was shared among all members of the family. They produced what they needed in their homes. Farm women made cloth for clothing and bedding using spinning wheels and hand looms. Some of them earned extra money as weavers producing cloth for yarn manufacturers. As farms became larger and more prosperous, farmers began hiring male laborers, who took over many of the tasks previously done by the women and children. Increasingly, farm women concentrated on household tasks and taking care of the children.

In the city, a similar thing happened. Families had once worked together making a product (shoes, for example) in their homes. In the new industrial society, middle-class women were expected to stay at home while their husbands went out to work. By 1840, "genteel" unmarried women had few career choices other than teacher, hatmaker, or dressmaker. Working-class women took on the work in mills and factories that had once been considered suitable for single "ladies." They also worked as maids, laundresses, nursemaids (nannies), and cooks.

Later in the century, as more women became better educated, they worked as doctors, lawyers, librarians, college professors, inventors, and architects. For many, though, it was a struggle to do what had been considered "men's work."

Some women did strike out on their own to do what they wanted, regardless of the barriers. Margaret Knight invented a machine for making square-bottomed paper bags. Mary Cassatt became a famous artist. Esther Howland manufactured valentines. Rebecca Lukens ran an iron mill. Maggie Lena Walker became the first woman bank president. As the century closed, more and more women were following in their brave footsteps.

"The Most Beautiful Sight"

Asa Candler, a soft drink manufacturer, once wrote, "The most beautiful sight we see is the child at labor." He wasn't talking about homework.

Child labor in the Victorian age was considered normal and necessary. Businessmen like Mr. Candler could pay working-class children lower wages than adults and boss them around more easily. Politicians knew that fast-growing industries needed cheap workers for 10- to 12-hour-a-day unskilled jobs. When factory owners broke the few child labor laws that did exist, politicians looked the other way.

Boys began their apprenticeship in a trade as early as the age of 10. As preteens, they went to war as drummer boys and buglers. They also carried drinking water to train passengers, sold newspapers, worked as night messengers and office boys, and toiled in the cotton mills and coal mines. Girls worked as street vendors selling matches, flowers, or hot corn, and as babysitters for their younger sisters and brothers while their parents worked. Farm children were expected to pitch in and were often hired out to other farmers.

Didn't children have to go to school? Not necessarily. In the first half of the century, parents who could afford it sent their children to private schools. State-funded, free public schools began opening in the 1830s. (Slave children weren't allowed to learn to read and write.) By 1889 most states had passed laws making it compulsory for children to go to school, although the laws weren't always enforced.

Boys and girls were burnt, cut, mangled, and poisoned in accidents on the job. But then, adults were burnt, cut, mangled, and poisoned on the job too. It wasn't until late in the century that children began to be treated as children rather than as small adults.

The Clock That Fired the Sun

In 1883 an Indianapolis newspaper editor complained, "The sun is no longer boss of the job. People must eat, sleep, and work as well as travel by railroad time."

In 1883, American and Canadian railroads set up four time zones across the two countries with an hour's difference between each zone. Some people who had followed "God's time" all their lives were outraged. Wasn't keeping track of time by the sun good enough anymore?

The problem for the railroads was that time was local and not exact. Even those who owned a clock or pocket watch set it by the sun. The earth's rotation around the sun meant that a town a few miles east of another town experienced sunrise, noon, and sunset earlier. This made it tricky for the railways to schedule their trains. When trains began racing the sun across the country, it became increasingly difficult. Charles Dowd's and Sir Sandford Fleming's time zone system solved the problem and is still in use today.

In the last part of the century, people's lives became more scheduled. Travelers had to arrive at the steamboat dock and railroad station "on time." Workers had to arrive at the factory, store, or office "on time." To do this, they needed to know the time "of-the-clock" (o'clock)— one o'clock, two o'clock, and so on.

In factory towns, factory owners kept track of the time for their workers. Six days a week they rang a bell (or set off a steam whistle) to get their workers up, rang it again to start the workday, and again to end the day. People who had previously heard only a church bell to call them to services on Sunday found that their days were now ruled by the strict, exact clock, not the easygoing sun.

Weird Job Titles of the 1800s

JIMMY DUCK—the sailor in charge of cleaning up the animal pens on board a ship

WOODHAWK—a man who sells wood to steamships

MULE SPINNER—a skilled textile worker who uses a spinning mule machine to do the same work that 100 workers once did using old-fashioned spinning wheels

TRAPPER BOY—a boy who opens and closes underground doors that "trap" fresh air in a coal mine

BULL WHACKER—a driver, also called a teamster, whose wagon is pulled by oxen

IRON PUDDLER—an ironworker who removes impurities from iron in a puddling furnace

Choosing a 19th-Century Career

Unlike today, Americans in the 1800s couldn't always choose the job they wanted to do, particularly if they were African Americans, Native Americans, immigrants, women, or poor adults or children. (You can figure out who's left.)

No one, of course, would choose to be a slave. The high demand for workers to plant and harvest the farm fields of the Americas fueled the African slave trade. About 12 million men, women, and children were taken from their homelands. Many died on the horrendous journey across the Atlantic in crowded ships. Bought by different slave traders and slaveholders, husbands were often separated from their wives and parents from their children, never to see one another again. After the American Revolution, slavery was still practiced in the South but was abolished in the North. Some Southern slaves bought their freedom or were freed by their owners, while others escaped to the North, Canada, or Mexico. Most, however, remained enslaved, with little choice in the jobs they were forced to do.

Let's pretend for a moment, though, that you could choose any of the jobs in this book. How would you go about applying for one? You could place a "Situation Wanted" ad in a local newspaper. Better still, you could ask your friends or relatives to recommend you for a job. "Who you know" is the fastest way to find a job in the 19th century. Just like today, employers want to see "references"—letters from past employers that say you did a good job. Looking clean and tidy for the interview is important too, although not necessary for dirty jobs such as digging canals. All set?

Turn the page!

CHAPTER 1

Exploration Jobs

Are you curious about what's on the other side of closed doors, rivers, or oceans? On early-19th-century maps, blank spaces stretched west from the Mississippi River. They were labeled *Unexplored Country* or *Immense Forests*, but what that really meant was "This Is One Big Fat Question Mark." It must have been exciting to point to that empty spot and say, "I'm going to be the first to go *here*."

Explorers made everyone proud. For a long time, most people ignored the fact that their heroes hadn't really been the "first." Meriwether Lewis and William Clark of the 1804 Corps of Discovery may have been the first Americans to explore the West all the way to the Pacific, but Spaniards and French Canadians had already poked around out there. Nor did the explorers travel without help from the folks who already lived in the West. Native people were usually happy to share their knowledge of their homeland with the new-comers—"If you go over that mountain pass, you'll find the river you're looking for." Explorers depended heavily on Native help to make their "discoveries."

THE FURRY HAT THAT CONQUERED THE WORLD

The furry hat that became a fashion fad in the 18th and 19th centuries was actually more fuzzy than furry. Hatmakers pressed cut-up beaver hairs into a waterproof material called felt, which could be shaped into a hat. A water-proof hat not only kept a man dry, but also said to the world, "I can afford this nice hat."

As the supply of beavers ran out in Europe, prices for their skins soared. They were so precious that the dirt on the floors of fur warehouses was sifted to retrieve every last hair. Fur traders needed a new supply of beaver pelts and turned to North America. As each creek was "beavered out," hunters traveled farther and farther west across the unexplored continent in search of furry gold.

Mountain Man

Mountain Woman

If you like camping, take a look at this 1822 newspaper ad: "To adventurous young men: Fur trading company wishes to hire one hundred men to go up the river Missouri to its source, where you will work for one, two, or three years."

Some Easterners think riding into the wilderness to trap pudgy little animals for hatmakers is the ultimate adventure. After you sign up, an experienced fur trapper shows "greenhorns" like you where to put the traps in a stream. You get used to wading up to your thighs in icy water to lay and check your traps.

Each summer, you and hundreds of other trappers make your way to the "rendezvous," a meeting place at the end of a trail. You hand in your few hundred pelts to the company trader and receive your pay. Because it takes two months for the traders' wagons to reach the rendezvous from the nearest town, the traders charge the trappers high prices for everything. After you've bought your supplies for the next trapping season and had a good time with your friends, you may find yourself penniless.

After 1840, men begin wearing silk hats and you're out of a job.

In the early years of the North American fur trade, many Native-American men trapped beaver to trade for guns, knives, cloth, and metal pots. As a fur trapper's wife, you go trapping with your husband. You help set up camp, gather firewood, cook, mend clothing, and skin and dry the beaver pelts. If you are the Indian wife of an American or French-Canadian mountain man, you have the same wilderness chores. You and your children travel with the trappers or stay with your family in the Indian village until your husband returns.

Sacagawea, the Shoshone wife of fur trader Toussaint Charbonneau, worked as an interpreter on the Lewis and Clark expedition. She introduced the explorers to her people and found wild plants and roots for everyone to eat along the way. Sacagawea was such a valuable member of the expedition that the explorers named a river in her honor.

Explorer

You are the leader of a government expedition sent to explore the Far West. No one has built any roads where you are going. You and your fellow soldiers will have to deal with dangerous rapids, steep mountain trails, swarms of mosquitoes, and bad weather. In just one day, Meriwether Lewis escaped from a grizzly bear and was charged by an angry buffalo. He woke up the next morning with a rattlesnake staring at him.

It obviously takes guts to be an explorer—in more ways than one. If the hunting is poor, you may be forced to eat bugs, skunks, candles, or even your horse. Explorers spend a lot of time "cleaning out their systems," thanks to their poor diets.

On your adventure, you write in a journal about the strange creatures and plants you see. You also collect animal skins, plants, and rocks for scientists to study back home.

Cartographer

It's your job to fill in the blanks on the maps with rivers, mountains, and trails. You might be hired by an explorer or by a fur trading company. With the help of instruments and mathematical tables, you pinpoint the longitude and latitude of the places you visit. You measure the heights of mountains and the widths of rivers. If you come across a landmark—something that sticks out—you mark that down too.

Charles Preuss, the mapmaker on John C. Frémont's 1842 expedition, was riding across the treeless Great Plains when he saw something weird—a forest. Aha, he thought, that's a good landmark. The next time he looked, the bushy trees were galloping away. His woods had turned into three immense herds of buffalo.

"Last night a stinker [skunk] was killed, and we ate it this morning for breakfast. I never thought such a foul-smelling beast could taste so good. During the attack it squirted right into Badeau's face; the fellow still smells of it ..."
— Charles Preuss, cartographer, 1842

18

CHAPTER 2

Frontier Jobs

Mountain men told wonderful stories around their campfires. When these tall tales made their way into the Eastern newspapers, readers found it difficult to believe even the true stories about buffalo stampedes, grizzly bear attacks, or hot springs. They enjoyed reading about the "Fur West," but they saw no need to go over the Appalachian Mountains to see it for themselves.

That all changed when a baby boom and immigration almost doubled the country's population between 1800 and 1820. Most people farmed for a living. Suddenly much of the farmland of the East was occupied. Young people, immigrants, and those looking for better opportunities began building new communities farther west. The frontier—the edge of American settlement— shifted into the lands of the Mississippi Valley and along the Great Lakes.

Storekeeper

People like to chat on your store's front porch or around the woodstove inside. You join in when you have a spare minute. You are an important person in the settlement. Your business is a community center, bank, and post office as well as a store.

On the shelves and counters, you put out spices, salt, sugar, tea, coffee, cocoa, candy, and salted fish and meat. The floor is lined with barrels and baskets. Turn one barrel's spigot and beer, molasses, or vinegar pours out. Raise the lid of another and scoop out flour, pickles, or crackers. Cloth, china, and kitchen utensils take up any space left over.

Your customers "barter" with you. You put a price on what you have to sell and they put a price on what they have to sell. Together, you come up with a fair trade. Sometimes your regular customers pay "on credit": you keep a list of the items they buy and ask them to pay just once or twice a year.

Frontier Farmer

You are a felling, grubbing, burning kind of guy during your first months on the frontier. To make way for your fields, you cut down ("fell") the trees with an ax, dig out roots and stones with a grubbing hoe, and then burn the brush and any logs you don't need. Next you plant the seeds brought from "back East" and build a one-room log cabin with a fireplace.

The corn, beans, squash, and potatoes that you plant are the same crops Native farmers grew here. The diseases brought by Europeans many years ago killed entire Indian villages, leaving thousands of acres of farmland unharvested. By the time you arrive, you can't even see the ghost fields—the forest has taken over.

When you aren't working in the fields, you cut wood for your woodpile, build fences, help your neighbors, and hunt wild animals and birds to stew in a pot over the fire. One of the birds you hunt is the passenger pigeon. Huge flocks of these tasty creatures sometimes darken the sky. They are so easy to shoot or catch with nets that by the end of the century they are almost all killed, mostly by professional hunters who sell the birds in the city markets. "Martha," the last of a few billion of her species, dies in a zoo in 1914.

In the early 1800s, you can't imagine such a thing happening. The forest and the food it provides seem endless—sometimes too endless as you struggle to clear your land.

"With $80 you will buy a quarter section of land … You will build a house with $50 … two horses will cost, with harness and plough, $100. Cows, and hogs, and seed corn, and fencing, with other expenses, will require the remaining $210. You would of course bring with you your sea bedding and store of blankets … and a good stock of wearing apparel."

— "Information and Advice to Emigrants to the United States: and from the Eastern to the Western States," John Melish, 1819

Frontier Farmer's Wife

You share the dream of a better life with your husband. While you're bent over a washtub scrubbing his dirty, smoky clothes, you might wonder for a moment when that life will begin. Most of the time, though, you just get on with it.

Before you know it, you're caring for children, feeding chickens, cooking meals, washing dishes, baking bread, hauling water, spinning yarn, weaving cloth, sewing clothes, grinding corn, milking cows, salting fish, churning butter, making soap, poking the fire, picking berries, weeding the garden, and helping your husband and neighbors. Whew! If you have six children—and many settlers do have large families—you line them up on "nail day" and clean and clip 120 nails.

"I made my first attempt at the washtub. Some of their clothing was literally black. I had no soft soap or lye, my only stool was too low, but I stuck to it resolutely till I got all laid in the last rinsing water ... sore back."
— Anna Briggs Bentley, Ohio pioneer, 1820s

SODDY SITE
In the last half of the century, farmers settling the treeless Great Plains built houses using strips of grassy earth called sod. You can visit the National Museum of American History's "Building a Sod House" site at http://american history2.si.edu/ourstoryinhistory/tryonline/buildsodhouse.html.

Peddler

You're a door-to-door salesman. On the frontier, though, the doors are miles apart. You ride a packhorse and sell tin utensils, thread, needles, buttons, pins, and pretty ribbon for "country pay"—the hides, homemade cloth, produce, and other items farm families have to trade. These you sell in town for two or three times what they cost you.

When better roads are built, you buy a horse and wagon, which you can fill with larger and heavier items. Your cart is today's dollar store. All your goods are inexpensive because your customers don't have much to trade.

The one thing you give away for free is news. Your customers love to hear what is happening in the neighboring townships. Because you're a regular visitor, they've probably given you a nickname. Let's hope it's not "Dewdrop," the nickname of a peddler who always had a disgusting drop hanging from the tip of his nose.

Schoolteacher

You stay with the families of your students during the school term. "Boarding round" makes it possible for the parents of a frontier community to hire you. Because you don't have to pay rent or buy your own food, they only have to pay you a dollar or two a week. You teach every day except Sunday.

Your one-room schoolhouse has a closet for storing lunch baskets, coats, and naughty children, but no washroom. You teach reading, writing, arithmetic, and a bit of history and geography. Paper is expensive, so your students write on their own personal blackboards, called slates.

You may be a farmer's son who has studied at a private academy (high school). In the winter, when your family doesn't need you on the farm, you teach. Beginning in May, a young woman takes over and you and the older boys work in the fields. By the end of the century, most teachers in grade schools are unmarried women who have studied at a teachers' college, teach year-round, and board with one family instead of several.

Miller

Everyone wants to help you build a gristmill in their township. Once farmers begin to grow more corn and wheat than they can use themselves, they want to sell or trade it for goods they need. They have too much grain to grind into flour by hand and they don't want to carry it to a distant mill over bumpy, stumpy roads anymore. Even a 10-mile (16 km) round trip can take all day.

Operating a mill is all turn, turn, turn. Water from a dammed stream or river turns the waterwheel. The waterwheel turns smaller wheels, which turn a big grindstone over a matching stationary stone. The sharp grooves on the stones grind the grain into flour. You must keep the grooves on your millstones sharp. If you don't, the flour will become sticky and make bad bread.

As the community grows, you may add a water-powered sawmill to your business. Boards, planks, and rafters for building houses, barns, and businesses are always in demand.

CHAPTER 3

Life and Death Jobs

People of this century were born at home rather than in a hospital. If they became ill, they were usually treated at home too. The hard physical work of young frontiersmen and women gave them the toned bodies of today's athletes. In some cases, a strong body helped them survive the many diseases the Victorian faced in a lifetime. Some parents didn't even name their babies until they were several months old because so many newborns died. Poor diets, too much alcohol, poor sanitation, ignorant "doctors," and poisonous "cures" all shortened people's lives.

Medical science could do little to fight disease and infection. No antibiotics existed. For much of the century, surgeons didn't know enough to wash their hands or sterilize their instruments and operating rooms. Doctors didn't understand how diseases spread. Epidemics of cholera, a severe bacterial infection caused by contaminated food and water, killed thousands in the 1830s and '40s. Most people accepted death as part of God's plan and "soldiered on," sad but trusting that their loved ones had gone to a better place.

Midwife

Don't you worry now. I've got everything to make it all come out right.

You help women give birth to their babies. It's hard work bringing a baby into the world, which is why it's called labor. You massage your client, make her cups of herbal tea, and do what you can to make her more comfortable. Then you help with the delivery.

Doctor

STRANGE "CURES"

Whooping cough:
Inhale the breath of
a fish.

Headache:
Place a buckwheat
pancake on your head.

Failing eyesight:
Shave your head.

Nosebleed:
Chew a newspaper.

Warts:
Rub warts with pebbles
and throw them into
a grave.

Your patients are very lucky if you've taken a 10-month medical school course and trained for two or three years with a local doctor. You may have simply apprenticed with a doctor or, if you are a "quack," had no training at all. No wonder your profession has such a poor reputation.

You make "house calls" on horseback. Most of your patients only send for you, though, when their own homemade cures don't work. They can't afford your visit and don't like the puking, peeing, pooing, or bleeding that often follow your arrival. You believe illness is caused by poisons in the fluids of a sick person's body. If you can get rid of some of the fluid, you'll get rid of the disease—or so the theory goes. You give your patients "gonna be sick" or "gotta go" medicines. You also "bleed" your patients,

making small cuts on their bodies with a knife or sticking bloodsucking worms called leeches onto their skin.

Not everyone thinks your treatments work (big surprise!). Homeopaths believe a kind word and a spoonful of their special medicine are just as good. Hydropaths are sure soaking in a hot bath will help. In the backcountry, people often turn to herb "doctors" and "grannies." These healers use Native American herb and root remedies as well as ones passed down in their own families. Sometimes they work and sometimes they don't.

By the 1860s, medical schools have stopped teaching bloodletting. You learn new ways to treat the sick, and the leeches go back to sucking on fish and swimmers' toes.

Pharmacist

Did you know that pharmacists like you invented two famous soft drinks in the 1800s? Both Coca-Cola and Pepsi-Cola began as fizzy medicines. You mix up similar liquid "tonics" and practice some "doctoring" too. Your customers ask you for remedies for their health problems and you sell them cough medicines, pain relievers, and laxatives. You also mix up medicines prescribed by doctors.

Your biggest competitors are sellers of "patent medicines." These peddlers are known as "snake-oil salesmen" because some claim that snake oil is the "special magical ingredient" in their "cure-alls." In fact, the most common ingredient of patent medicines is alcohol. Even "soothing syrups" for fussy babies contain it. Until the Pure Food and Drug Act is passed in 1906, they are free to make any claim they want about their products. "Cures man or beast!" is a popular one. Possible side effects—addiction, for example—never have to be mentioned.

I hope this cures 'em.

Horse/Cow Doctor

In the first half of the century, farmers get in touch with you when their animals are sick or hurt. You know a little bit about animals, probably because you once worked as a blacksmith's helper or a wagon driver. But you know very little about animal diseases. You just pretend you do.

Sorry, Bessy. This is for your own good.

Your cures sometimes make your patients worse. Bleeding a horse or cow is one of your most popular treatments. Farmers believe that if it helps humans, it should help animals. You also pour "medicine" down the animals' throats. It may contain everything from pepper to the animals' own pee!

If the horse or cow lives, you take the credit. If it dies, you shake your head sadly and say that the farmer didn't send for you soon enough. Horses and cows are happy when trained veterinarians take over their care later in the century.

Coffin Maker

You are the local carpenter or cabinetmaker. Coffins are a sideline. When someone dies, you stop making furniture and build a simple wooden box. A woman who "lays out" bodies for a fee comes to the family home. She washes and dresses the corpse for burial in the coffin you have made. The sexton, who looks after the church and its graveyard, digs the grave and rings the church bell before the funeral service.

Around the 1830s, some cabinetmakers, livery stable keepers, and sextons begin "undertaking" the entire funeral, from preparing the body to supplying the coffin and hearse. Instead of becoming an undertaker, you decide to open a coffin shop. You still make simple pine boxes for poor clients. Your wealthier customers, though, can order a beautifully carved coffin for their "dearly departed."

Being buried alive couldn't happen today, but some people in the 1800s worried about it, particularly after reading Edgar Allan Poe's scary stories. Inventors took out patents on "life-preserving coffins." Some had lids that would pop open if the "person in a trance" moved during the funeral service. The well-named Albert Fearnaught invented the "Grave-Signal," a flag that waved above-ground if the accidentally buried person tugged a rope. Few of these weird caskets were ever used.

Youth behold and shed a tear,
Fourteen children slumber here.
See their image how they shine
Like flowers of a fruitful vine.
— Epitaph on a gravestone

CHAPTER 4

Artisan Jobs

Artisans (also called craftsmen or mechanics) included the butcher, the baker, the candlestick maker, the gunsmith, the brewer, and anyone else who worked at a skilled trade. They fell in the middle of society, between upper-class "gentlemen"—rich merchants and large landowners, for example—and lower-class laborers and servants.

These men, who played an important role in both old and frontier communities, took great pride in their work. Like Native craftspeople, they considered it their duty to pass along the complex skills of their craft to the next generation. In the 1700s and early 1800s, boys became apprentices to master artisans in exchange for a bed, meals, clothing, and some basic education. At the age of 21 they became "journeymen," trained workers who were paid for each completed item. They continued to work and learn alongside the masters until they too became masters with their own small workshops.

Basket Maker

Your mother taught you how to weave strips of bark and branches into baskets. In your Native-Californian culture, woven plant material is the plastic of today; it's difficult to look around and not see something made of it. As well as baskets, you weave trays, bowls, dishes, watertight cups, sieves, animal and fish traps, toys, and baby carriers. You also make baskets for special ceremonies, decorating them with brightly colored feathers, beads, and shells.

Blacksmith

In this horse-and-buggy era, you shoe the horse and often fix the buggy.

To make horseshoes, you soften a bar of iron in the charcoal fire burning in your forge. When the iron is white-hot, you lift it out with big tongs and place it on your anvil. Quickly, before the iron cools and hardens again, you hammer it into the shape of a horseshoe, then drop it into a bucket of water to temper, or harden, it.

The next step is to nail the new horseshoes onto the horse's feet. Don't worry—this doesn't hurt the horse, because its hooves are like giant toenails. Shoeing horses does, however, take practice and a gentle voice and touch. If you're not careful, a kick from a frightened young horse can send you flying across the shop.

Blacksmiths also make tools, kitchen utensils, and new parts for wagons, carriages, sleighs, and plows. Everyone likes to visit the "smithy," your workshop. You're the hottest and noisiest show in town. Tap-tap-tap, CLANG! Tap-tap-tap, CLANG! Hammers crash, sparks fly, arms swing, sweat pours. Before their eyes, you and your assistant turn a piece of iron into something they can use.

Wheelwright

You are a carpenter who makes wooden wagon and buggy wheels. It helps to be strong so that you can drive the spokes into the hub with your large, heavy hammer. The local blacksmith makes the iron strips for your rims, unless you do your own "ironing."

You sometimes build wagons, too, or team up with the blacksmith to make horse-drawn sleighs. Your shop is close to the blacksmith and, if you're smart, not far from the local hotel. Travelers frequently break their wagons or wheels on the rough roads and are always happy to see a wheelwright's repair sign.

Cooper

You sit on a horse and shave for hours every day with a knife. Fortunately for you, the "horse" is a bench that you sit on, and you shave pieces of wood, not your hairy face. You could be a wet cooper, who makes watertight oak barrels to hold liquids; or a dry cooper, who makes barrels for dry foods, china, and nails; or a white cooper, who makes pails, buckets, and tubs.

Businesses that ship their goods overseas or across the country need as many barrels as you can make. You're so busy that you hire local farmers to cut rough staves for you in the winter, which your journeymen finish in the barrel works. In the 1830s, cardboard boxes and packages appear, followed by cheap metal containers, and your customers begin to disappear.

Butcher

At the livestock market outside the city, you pick out the healthiest cattle or pigs, walk them to your house, and slaughter them in the backyard. You might want to keep some bandages handy, because you use very sharp knives and cleavers to kill the animals and cut up their carcasses.

Each workday, before the sun rises, you load the meat into a wheelbarrow or horse-drawn cart and take it to your stall in the public market building. You wear a top hat and gentleman's clothing, protected by a spotless white apron. (After all, you are a skilled tradesman and a respectable businessman.) Sometimes you march with other butchers in a "fat-beef" parade, showing off very fat, prize-winning steers or decorated carts of meat to potential customers.

If you want to become rich, why not think about opening a large slaughter- and meat-packing house next to a river? You can sell the leftover fat (tallow) to soap- and candle-makers and the hides to leather tanners. Your workers sweep the manure, blood, and unusable scraps into the water. By the 1840s, some city rivers are slimy sewers.

CHAPTER 5
Factory and Mill Jobs

How would you feel if you passed one school grade but weren't allowed to enter the next one? What if this happened to you year after year? This is what began happening to journeymen.

As farmers became more successful, they bought more goods from stores. Some artisans and merchants expanded their businesses to keep up with the demand. They invested in new machinery, bigger buildings, and more workers. They also began changing the way craftsmen worked.

Traditionally, masters paid their journeymen for each completed product—a shoe, a wheel, a barrel. A journeyman sold his product, not himself. That changed when masters began paying wages and pushing craftspeople to work harder, faster, and for less money. Journeymen were no longer able to save enough money to open a competitive workshop themselves. Instead, they became factory wage-earners working *for* the master instead of *with* him. They became members of the working class rather than the middle class.

Seamstress

You work at home sewing shirts by hand. A tailor or journeyman tailor designs the shirt, makes the pattern, picks out the fabric and buttons, and cuts the cloth. You pick up a bundle of precut pieces from the clothing factory and sew them together. Like all women, you learned how to sew as a girl, so your "piecework" is considered unskilled. However, since sewing is women's work, it is also considered respectable.

It takes 20,000 tiny stitches to make a man's shirt. Working 12 to 14 hours a day, you can make about seven shirts a week for 12 cents a shirt. If the tailor doesn't like your work, he can take the finished shirt but refuse to pay you. When you don't have any work, you may have to depend on charity just to survive or to feed your family if you're a single mother with children who are too young to work.

Mill Worker

In the 1820s, you are one of many New England farm girls who have come to work as unskilled laborers in a water-powered cotton mill. You are excited to be away from your family for nine to ten months, making your own money and having an adventure before you marry.

The mill is a very respectable place or your parents wouldn't have allowed you to come. You have a curfew, live in a company-owned boardinghouse, and must go to church every Sunday. The clanging factory bell calls you to work at sunrise. From then until sunset, you operate a machine that spins cotton fibers into yarn. You replace empty bobbins of "roping" (fiber) with full ones, tie up threads that break, and stop the machine to "doff" (remove) spools full of finished yarn. In the evening you read or write letters home. Sometimes you go to an "improvement circle" with your friends at the local church, where you listen to a lecturer or write articles or poems for the mill girls' literary magazine.

At bedtime, you crawl into the bed you share with another mill girl and say good night to your roommates in the bed across the room. After the loud clattering of the machinery all day, you enjoy the quiet—until Lucy begins to snore.

THE KISS OF DEATH

Imagine you have to take a breath through a straw every eight minutes for twelve hours. Then imagine your sick little sister used the same straw just yesterday. Mill girls who were weavers had to stop their looms frequently to change an empty bobbin of thread for a full one. To thread their shuttles—the device that carried the woof thread back and forth between the warp threads—they sucked the thread from the new bobbin through a hole in the shuttle. Along with the thread, they inhaled lung-damaging lint and picked up contagious germs. The "kiss-of-death shuttle" made many workers sick.

Shoemaker

You learned your craft in an old-time shoe shop, which produced custom-made boots for men and buttoned or laced shoes for women. Today your own shop is much different. You never wear a leather apron or teach journeymen how to make shoes anymore. Dressed in the expensive suit of a businessman, you spend your time finding new places to sell your factory's ready-made shoes and figuring out cheaper ways to manufacture them.

One way to keep costs down is to divide the shoemaking into simple steps, with each worker doing only one task. No one learns how to make an entire shoe anymore. Men called clickers cut the leather with a clicking knife. Women and children stitch together the "uppers" and linings of the shoes at home. Journeymen fit the uppers over a foot-shaped wooden form called a last and attach them to the soles. Apprentices, who are paid a wage to deliver pieces and collect sewn shoe parts, learn nothing about the art of shoemaking.

Your journeymen are unhappy, but you don't care. You can hire immigrant shoe workers, who are willing to work for lower wages and longer hours than the bitter journeymen.

"Where we have to sit on our seats from twelve to sixteen hours per day, to earn one dollar, it must be apparent to all that we are in a sad condition."
—William Frazier, shoe worker, mid-1840s

Glassblower

Machinist

If you like blowing soap bubbles, you might want to think about becoming a glassblower. From ancient times, people have thought of glass-blowers as magicians.

You work in a glass factory. After the "melter" turns sand and ashes into molten glass in his melting furnace, he fills a large pot for you. The "gatherer" dips your blowpipe into the pot and covers the end with a "gob" of molten glass. You blow the gob into a window, bottle, or other object. Except for the word "gob," how much more magical could a job be?

To be fair, this is tough, thirsty work, particu-larly if you are working 32 pounds (15 kg) of glass at the end of your blowpipe to make a windowpane. Making bottles is easier. You gather a small gob on the blowpipe, puff a bubble into it, drop the lump into an iron mold, which a small boy opens and closes, and blow the glass into its fixed shape. By the end of the century, bottle-making machines will be turning out 1,800 bottles an hour compared to your 25.

Being a blacksmith is hard, physical labor and seems a little old-fashioned to you. You were trained as a machinist in a machine shop, where mechanical rather than hand tools are used to shape metal. Mill and factory owners who don't have an in-house machinist ask you to fix or replace their broken machines.

While repairing a machine, you might suggest ways that it could be improved. If your suggestion cuts costs or speeds up production, the factory owner will usually want to try it out. In the machine shop, you use steam- or water-driven filing and drilling machines to shape machine parts from pieces of metal. You need only six hours to do what it took six days to do with hammer, chisel, and file at the beginning of the century.

Like the butcher, you arrive at work wearing a top hat and suit. No one worries about worker safety. You don't wear safety goggles or safety boots, and you sometimes have to be rescued by a co-worker when your flowing black tie gets stuck in a machine.

On-the-Water Jobs

As settlers moved farther inland from the Atlantic coast, often using rivers as their highways, others stayed behind to continue making their living from the sea. Wealthy merchants sent their fleets of sailing ships across the oceans and up and down the coast to trade what Americans had for what they didn't have. How about some tree trunks for tea? Or some fish for watches?

In the 1820s, steamboats carrying farm produce from the newly settled frontier puffed their way along the Mississippi to New Orleans. Dockworkers loaded the steamers' cargoes onto ships for the final leg of their journey up to the northern cities. The ships returned south with their holds loaded with factory goods. With the 1825 opening of the Erie Canal connecting Lake Erie and the Hudson River, horse-pulled barges cut the journey to and from the East in half.

Cut-tail

You're a teenager hired as cut-tail and cook on a small fishing schooner heading for the Grand Banks off Newfoundland. Over the next two or three months at sea, the half-dozen fishermen on board teach you how to fish for cod with a hook and line. Cod are big fish—30 to 40 pounds (14 to 18 kg). You wear fingerless woolen gloves called "nippers" to protect your hands from the sharp line as you haul in your catch. Your pay is based on the number of fish you catch, so you proudly notch the tail of each one you land to show that it's yours.

Shipbuilder

If you like drawing and making models, this might be a good job for you. Each new ship begins as a wooden model. Of course, you can't just walk into the shipyard and say you want to design and build ships. You must first apprentice as a ship's carpenter, then work your way up to journeyman shipwright, and, finally, to master builder and owner of your own "yard."

A shipyard is like a noisy factory set up near the sea. Every worker has a job that plays a part in making one product, in this case a ship. You hire axmen to turn round logs into square timbers. You hire sawyers to make planks, caulkers to make the seams of the hull watertight, and spar makers to make the masts and spars that hold up the sails. Carpenters, blacksmiths, cabinetmakers, riggers, sailmakers, and unskilled laborers complete your team.

At the launch of the ship, all your workers and half the town gather at the yard. The excited crowd shouts, "There she goes!" as the hull slips into the water. It's a great moment. Your boat floats.

Ship Biscuit Maker

Stays crisp and fresh for months at sea!

People say your crackers are so hard that they have to be dipped in tea before they can be eaten. Does this bother you? Not a bite. You can't help it if your flour-water-salt-and-a-bit-of-fat biscuits become stale after a few weeks in a barrel.

All the merchants whose ships sail out of the Atlantic ports need cheap biscuits that won't get moldy on long voyages. They often force their sailors to live on salt pork, fish, potatoes, and your "hardtack." Sometimes the crackers are mushed up with water and a spoonful of molasses. This yucky dish is called—you guessed it—mush.

Your customers are the shipowners, not the sailors, so why should you care if your crackers must be mushed because they can't be cracked? By mid-century your bakery has become a factory. Its machines turn out thousands of crackers, not only for ships but for general stores and wagon trains, too.

Lighthouse Keeper

You live in a lighthouse, alone, or with your family, if you are married. It might be perched on a remote island or on upright wooden poles (pilings) in the middle of a bay. For months at a time you may not see another person or, if fog sets in, much of anything. It may take you half a day to sail to the nearest town in your skiff, a small boat that can be sailed or rowed.

The most important part of your job is lighting the wicks of the oil lamps at the top of the tower each night. You must keep the lamps full of whale oil and the reflectors and windows spotless. No weekends off. No holidays. Ships depend on your light to guide them safely into the harbor. You can't let them down.

Some 19th-century "wickies" became famous for their daring rescues at sea. Ida Lewis took over from her father as keeper of a Rhode Island lighthouse. During her career, she pulled drowning adults, children, and even a prize sheep into the station boat. Not baa-aaa-d!

Dory Fisherman

Later in the century, fishing schooners carry eight 16-foot-long (5 m) rowboats, called dories. At the fishing grounds, you help lower the dories overboard at dawn and climb into one. Fishermen in dories can cover a larger area and catch more fish than men fishing from a schooner.

You fish standing up, a line in each hand. If the fish are biting, you work hard for three or four hours until the skipper blows a horn. Then you row over to the ship and pitch your fish up onto the deck.

After lunch, you fish until about three in the afternoon, toss up your fish, have supper, and begin "dressing down." That's not taking off your clothes and putting on your jammies; it's cleaning the catch. You work in a team of three—a throater, who cuts off the heads; a gutter, who pulls out the insides; and a splitter, who slices the fish lengthwise, ready for salting. After all the fish are dressed, you have a "mug up" (a cup of tea) and go to bed—except if it's your turn to stand watch.

Whaleboat Boatheader

As the four oarsmen row quietly towards the whale, you stand in the stern of the 30-foot-long (9 m) whaleboat and steer with a long oar. Whales are good listeners: one splash of your oar can "gally" (frighten) your prey into a dive. You brace yourself as the harpooner throws his harpoon into the whale's back. Then the exciting part of your job begins. The harpoon line attaches the boat to the whale. As the crew is pulled by the injured animal through the waves, you must keep the boat from swamping and be quick to handle any sudden change of course. New England whalers call this wild ride the "Nantucket Sleighride."

Once the whale tires out, you kill it with a lance and your crew hauls it back to the ship. "Blubbermen" cut up the whale into pieces. You help throw the blubber into huge try-pots, where it is "tried out," or boiled down, to make oil. Whaling ships look as if they're on fire, the smelly smoke hiding their masts and rigging. The valuable oil, which is used in lamps and to lubricate machines, is poured into barrels and stored belowdecks. The fingernail-like baleen from the whale's mouth will be sold to makers of umbrella ribs, skirt hoops, and corsets (the tightly tied underwear that makes Victorian women look "wasp-waisted").

Steamboat Pilot

Canal Hoggee

As a pilot, you have to be an expert at "reading" the river from the wheelhouse perched on top of your three-decker steamboat. See those fine lines fanning out across the surface in the distance? They're made by a hidden sandbar that could ground your boat. To avoid it, you must turn your giant steering wheel as quickly as you can. (The great size of the wheel magnifies your muscle power and gives you enough force to turn the boat's rudder.) Narrow channels, dead trees, and rapids test your navigation skills as well. Despite all these hazards, a steamboat in the 1820s can go 100 miles (160 km) a day upstream. With steam powering your paddle wheels, you speed past the old-fashioned keel-boats. Pushed along with poles, they manage a poky 20 miles (32 km) a day.

It is only fair to warn you, though, that steamboats have a nasty habit of blowing up. Before 1850, boiler explosions on 150 American steamboats will kill nearly 1,500 passengers and crew members. The firemen in the engine rooms probably cause some of these explosions. Firemen like to race other steamboats. Some of them tape down the safety valves on their boilers to make the paddle wheels turn faster.

You are the least important worker on the new canals, but without you, the boats wouldn't move. Canal boats are towed by two or three horses that walk along a towpath beside the canal. Your job is to lead the horses for about four hours at a time; then another driver and team take over. Sometimes the relief horses are kept on board and sometimes they are waiting in a shed along the way.

Like you, many hoggees are boys, some as young as 12. Most of the time, the captain is telling you to hurry up, so you look forward to stopping for a while at a lock—one of the watery "steps" inside gates that let boats move up- or downhill. As your canal boat waits its turn, you sing with the crews of the other barges in line. Your favorite song is "The Raging Canal." You particularly like the lines, "We trusted to our driver, although he was but small, for he knew all the windings of that raging canal." (Probably best not to think about a later verse where he and his team fall into the canal during a storm and the horses drown.)

CHAPTER 7

Going West Jobs

Horace Greeley, a journalist and supporter of Western settlement once wrote, "Go west, before you are fitted for no life but that of the factory." Between 1840 and 1860, nearly 300,000 migrants took his advice. Some planned to buy cheap government farmland, some hoped to use their skills in new communities, some were trying to escape religious or racial persecution, and others wanted to strike it rich.

In 1848 a sea captain returned to Boston with a bag of gold from the newly annexed Territory of California. Rumors spread that gold nuggets the size of eggs could be picked up on the river bottoms. Thousands of people left their jobs behind and headed west to seek their fortunes.

Stonemason

You are a Chinese stonemason who has arrived in San Francisco in the 1850s. The growing population of California during the gold rush has caused a building boom. Suddenly, building materials are very hard to find. Merchants begin shipping prefabricated buildings in pieces from the East Coast around Cape Horn. Other "pre-fabs" come from across the Pacific.

Your job is to put up a building with granite blocks precut in China and shipped across the ocean. Like other masons, you are highly skilled. You know how to shape stone by hand with chisels and hammers, how to take measurements, how to make and mix mortar, and, most importantly, how to build walls that won't fall down. When you and your fellow Chinese masons learn that you are being paid less than American masons, you go on strike in 1852.

Wagon Train Leader

You may be a former mountain man hired to guide overlanders traveling west on the overland trails. Or you could be a migrant yourself who has been elected wagon boss by the other men in your group.

Before you start out across the Great Plains in May, you try to talk Albert out of loading a heavy oak table into his covered wagon. You've heard stories about furniture, china dishes, and even a piano left on the side of the trail, the oxen or mules too tired to haul them any farther. When everyone is set to go, you yell "Fall-l-l-l in!" The 50 or so wagons line up behind you to begin the five- to six-month-long adventure.

Each day at noon, you call a stop for the long lunch break called "nooning." Like everyone else, you turn your oxen and cows loose to graze. After lunch, the men hunt or fish while the women and children collect buffalo "chips," sun-dried buffalo dung used as fuel for the campfire.

At dusk, you stop the wagon train again and "circle up." Alternate wagons swing left or right to form a circle. Campfires are lit. You eat dinner and make sure you have enough men standing guard that night. (Native people often guide migrants or trade with them, but the occasional attack has created widespread fear.) As you crawl into your tent beside the wagon, you're happy that the wagon train has gone 15 miles (24 km) that day.

Almost there, folks.

Military Post Commander

Welcome to the land of opportunity, fine settlers.

As a military officer, you've led patrols of soldiers escorting wagon trains through Indian land. Now you're in charge of a fort set up by the federal government on the Oregon Trail to help establish the government's authority over the region.

Some of the migrants who reach your isolated post need your help. You authorize the post doctor to treat civilians with signs of cholera, injuries from falling under wagons, and snakebite. The fort's blacksmith and carpenter can't help everyone whose wagon has broken or whose ox has thrown a shoe. You rent out their equipment at night so that desperate overlanders can make their own repairs. The most needy are usually those who are returning east after running out of supplies. You give them what they need from the fort's store for their sad journey home.

GOING WEST PANTS

The people who made the most money during the gold rush were those who sold supplies to the miners. German immigrant Levi Strauss made his fortune by designing and selling hard-wearing work pants to miners and, later, cowboys. The miners called them "levis." Today we call them "jeans."

Prospector

You're a long way from home. You could be an experienced miner from Mexico or Chile, an African-American freedman, or a hopeful gold seeker from eastern North America, Europe, or China.

You pan for gold in the mountain stream on your claim, the piece of public land that you have legally "claimed" as yours to mine. You dig out some gravel from the bottom or bank, put it in a tin pan, and sift out the lighter stones, leaving the heavier gold grains behind. When all the gold is panned out of the streams, you team up with other miners and build long wooden trays called "Long Toms." You use these to wash larger amounts of gravel, often for smaller amounts of gold. You dig and sift all day long. Most of your hard-earned gold is spent on food and supplies.

Only 5 out of every 100 forty-niners (those taking part in the 1849 gold rush) are women. Some happily mine alongside their husbands, while others only visit the diggings. After her first day of panning for gold, one woman decided she had had enough: "I wet my feet, tore my dress, spoilt a pair of new gloves, nearly froze my fingers, got an awful headache, took cold and lost a valuable breastpin."

Boardinghouse Operator

Many gold miners will pay top dollar for anything home-cooked. Your small fruit pies sell for a dollar apiece. Soon you're earning more than some miners and decide to open a boardinghouse.

You cook meals, make beds, and do the laundry for your boarders. If you're doing well, you hire another woman to help you. At mid-century many people live in boardinghouses in the cities. In the Atlantic ports, you can hire "runners" to go down to the docks and persuade sailors and newly arrived immigrants to come to your boardinghouse. In California, though, when your boarders hear news of a rich gold or silver strike somewhere else, your house can empty in a day. You may have to close up and move too.

Some free African-American women traveled west on their own. They worked as cooks on freight wagon trains or as laundresses. During the gold rush, black women ran several popular boardinghouses.

Laundress

During the gold rush, you run a successful business washing men's clothes. In the days before washing machines, doing the laundry is long, hard work, usually women's work.

Here's how to do it: haul water in pails from a lake, creek, or well. Fill a large washtub. Use a washboard to scrub the dirt out of the clothes with soap. Boil the clothes in an iron pot over a fire, then rinse them in another pot. After wringing out the wet clothes, hang them to dry. Heat up the heavy iron over a fire and press out wrinkles. Repeat last step many times.

In 1825, Hannah Montague of Troy, New York, became so tired of washing her husband's shirts when only the collar was dirty that she invented a detachable collar. Less imaginative women who could afford it hired a laundress.

Burp!

Belch

Hicc

up

Forced Laborer

As a Native American, you do the hard, dirty work that Anglo Californians don't want to do. Under an 1850 state law, you have been arrested for being a dangerous "vagrant"—this is someone who doesn't have a job and is considered a public nuisance. In your case, the law is an excuse for forcing you to work on a farm or in a mine. Native children are also seized and forced to work.

A group of kidnappers with nine children under the age of 10 once claimed that they had taken the children as "an act of charity" because their parents had been killed. They were asked how they knew the parents were dead. "I killed some of them myself," replied one man.

By 1870 the Native-American population of California had fallen to 30,000 from about 150,000 in 1848, as a result of racial violence, forced labor, and epidemics.

WESTERING WITHOUT HOPE

A gold rush in the Appalachian foothills of Georgia in 1829 and the greed of American settlers pushed the Cherokee people off their homeland. The Cherokee successfully farmed land that white farmers wanted for themselves. After the government passed the Removal Act in 1830, the army forced the people of the Cherokee Nation to move west to "Indian Territory" (now Oklahoma). The Cherokee called the route they followed the Trail of Tears.

CHAPTER 8

Traveling-Here-and-There Jobs

If the catwhipper is coming to your house, do you hide with Kitty in the barn? Not if you want any shoes, you don't. In this century a few traveling shoemakers known as "catwhippers" still made yearly visits to rural customers who lived far from the nearest shoemaker. They set up a portable bench in the farmhouse kitchen and made new shoes or patched ones that "still had wear in 'em."

Many workers traveled here and there, particularly in the first half of the century. If farmers disliked butchering their own animals, they could hire a traveling butcher. Circuit preachers rode on horseback visiting settlers on the remote frontier. Colporteurs sold Bibles and religious literature door to door. In the cities, hackmen, the era's cab drivers, picked up passengers in their carriages while street sellers walked about selling everything from wood to muffins.

Swindlers, also called sharpers or hucksters, moved quickly through an area, preying on people's hopes and fears. They sold products or services that didn't live up to their promises: amazing seeds "found in an Egyptian tomb," apple trees that would produce half sweet and half sour apples, and powders that would prevent oil lamps from blowing up.

Stagecoach Driver

Circuit Lawyer

With a team of four strong horses pulling your stagecoach filled with paying passengers, you can really "cut dirt" along a good road. All other traffic has to pull off to the side to let you through. Most of the time, though, your nine passengers bounce around inside the coach while the several seated on top "hold on for dear life." Potholes and ruts in muddy roads can slow you down, break wheels, and even overturn the stage. About every 12 miles (19 km), you stop at a relay station and quickly change your team for a new one. At the stops along the stage line, you drop off and pick up passengers and deliver mail and newspapers.

In the West, you drive for the Wells Fargo express company. You often carry gold and silver from the mines to the banks back East. Don't worry about robbers: armed guards "ride shotgun" with you to prevent any outlaws from stealing your green strongboxes.

"The best seat in a stage is the one next to the driver. If the team runs away—sit still and take your chances. If you jump, nine out of ten times you will get hurt. Don't smoke a strong pipe inside the coach—spit on the leeward side. Don't lop [hang] over neighbors when sleeping … Don't grease your hair, because travel is dusty."
— "Tips for Stage Riders," *Omaha Herald*, 1877

In the spring and fall, you travel with the judges and other lawyers of the circuit court, which finds people accused of crimes innocent or guilty. The court opens in the largest town of its district and then makes "the swing" around the countryside. You feel like part of a traveling circus. Farmers and villagers crowd into the courtrooms to watch the legal dramas unfold.

Some of the judges you work with may seem a bit strange. Theophilus Parsons was known for not caring about his appearance. His wife bugged him about it, so he promised her that he would put a clean shirt on every day of the next circuit. And he did. He just didn't bother taking off the shirt he had worn the previous day.

If you want to become a politician, being a circuit lawyer is a good way to meet lawyers, businessmen, and other important people who might help you get elected. Abraham Lincoln was a circuit lawyer and he didn't do too badly.

Lightning Rod Man

Sure to save livestock and loved ones!

You are good at "humbugging"—persuading people that they need your product. You tell farmers that a bolt of lightning struck Jedadiah Brown's barn in the next county. The fire spread to the house, where Jedadiah, his wife, his 10 sons, his poor sick Mama, and Mutt, the family dog, were sleeping. Of course, none of this is true, but your tall tale does the trick. You sell farmers so many rods that their houses and barns look like porcupines.

The farmers could protect their buildings by putting up one or two rods themselves at a fraction of what you charge, but you convince them that your rods are very special. They aren't like the rod Benjamin Franklin invented way back in 1749. Your modern, specially installed lightning rod even protects against tornadoes. Pure humbug!

Limner

In the days before photography, having a portrait painted was the only way people could record what they or their loved ones looked like. Well-known artists such as John Singer Sargent or James Abbott McNeill Whistler, who painted a famous picture of his mother, often painted portraits for rich clients.

As a limner, it is unlikely that your work will ever make you famous or rich. Most limners travel from village to village painting so-so portraits. James Guild, a folk artist in the 1820s, had this to say about one of his paintings: "It looked more like a strangled cat than it did like her."

If you have James's problem, you can always become a silhouette-cutter. You ask your customer to sit sideways, hold up a piece of black paper, and cut out the profile of his or her head with a pair of scissors. If you can't do this "by eye," you use a candle to cast your subject's shadow onto a screen. You trace the shadow onto white paper, cut it out, and trace it onto black paper. Silhouette-cutting pays much less than portrait painting, but you can set up a booth at county fairs and do a snipping good business.

CHAPTER 9

Sweet-Tooth Jobs

In these jobs, you either satisfy a person's sweet tooth or repair the damage caused by it.

Sugar Plantation Owner

Your life is sweet, although you do work hard. You live in a beautiful house full of expensive furniture, china, and paintings. Your wife dresses in the latest fashions and wears sparkling necklaces and earrings. Your children are never asked to set the table or make their beds. You are a member of the South's planter class—the wealthy people who grow cotton, rice, tobacco, and sugar on plantations.

You need a large workforce to plant, grow, and cut your sugarcane, and to work in your mill, crushing the juice from the cane and boiling it down into sugar. Like other planters, you rely on the labor of men, women, and children who cannot choose another way of life. You buy and sell slaves, supervise their work in the fields and mill, and look after shipping the brown sugar to northern sugar refineries, where it is made into white sugar. Your plantation makes even more money after you start using the invention of a free man of color, Norbert Rillieux.

Rillieux's father was a Louisiana sugar planter and his mother a slave. After Norbert was born, his father declared him free and, when his son grew up, sent him to Paris to be trained as an engineer. After watching slaves boiling sugarcane juice in large open kettles and pans on his father's plantation, Norbert invented an evaporator that not only produced better sugar but also made it much less dangerous to make.

ALL-NATURAL CHEWING GUM
Native Americans and lumberjacks often chopped off bits of spruce gum to chew. (Don't try this in your local woods.) The first American chewing gum, Maine Pure Spruce Gum, was made in Bangor, Maine, in 1848.

Maple Syrup Producer

Native people taught 18th-century settlers in eastern North America how to make maple syrup and sugar. Imported sugar was expensive, so the pioneers were happy to find a sweetener they could make themselves. In the 1800s, your customers can buy American-made sugar or molasses. For a special treat, though, they still like the unique taste of the maple syrup you make on your farm.

In February or March, you head out into the snowy "sugar bush" to tap the maple trees. You drill a hole into each tree, stick in a spout, and hang a wooden bucket beneath it. Over the next six weeks, each tree will produce about three or four bucketfuls of sap.

The collected sap is boiled down into syrup in a huge iron pot hung over a wood fire. It takes 40 gallons (150 liters) of sap to make 1 gallon (4 liters) of maple syrup. The syrup is boiled down again to make sugar. At your "sugaring-off" party, you spoon out warm sugar onto fresh snow to make taffy for your guests to eat.

Candy Maker

According to you, it doesn't take much skill to make penny candy sticks. You just boil down some sugar and water in a huge copper kettle, knead 15 pounds (7 kg) of the sticky mass on your marble table, pull and twist it on the pulling hook, press a flavored stripe into the batch, twist and pull it again, and then cut it into sticks with giant scissors. This takes muscle, not a true confectioner's skill. But the light-as-air marshmallows made from the root sap of the marshmallow plant, the creamy creams, the spun caramel baskets—these are works of art.

By the end of the century you are hiring water-color artists to decorate your most expensive candy with tiny paintings. (Your customers don't seem to worry about eating paint.) Big candy manufacturers, on the other hand, are using machines to churn out thousands of cheap candies. They promote handing out candy on Halloween. Children don't care if it's just a clever way to sell more of their sweet treats.

Hokey-pokey Seller

This is a yelling and selling job. Every city street vendor has a "cry," such as "Here comes the fish man, bring out your dishpan!" or "Hot corn! Here's your lily-white hot corn!" In the summer, you push a wheelbarrow along the streets, yelling "Hokey-pokey, pokey ho!" (Okay, it's a bit silly, but better than that annoying tune today's ice-cream trucks play.) "Hokey-pokey" is just another name for cheap ice cream or ice milk. You sell a small block of it on a square of brown paper for a penny, mostly to children.

"Hokey-pokey, penny a lump
The more you eat, the more you jump."
— Skipping rhyme

Dentist

Some people pull their own rotten teeth after reading the instructions in a home remedy book. Ouch! Other, less brave people make their painful way to a doctor or even the local black-smith, barber, or pharmacist. By 1830, though, most large cities have trained dentists, while rural areas are served by traveling dentists.

You clean your patients' teeth, fill cavities with gold foil, and pull out teeth. Sometimes you try to replace the pulled tooth. Happily, no one transplants teeth from corpses anymore; you use porcelain (china) teeth instead. Usually the fake tooth falls out and you end up tying it to the remaining teeth. You also fit porcelain dentures.

Naturally, you don't enjoy causing pain each time you pull a tooth. A fellow dentist, Horace Wells, volunteers in 1844 to have one of his own teeth pulled after inhaling the newly discovered "laughing gas" (nitrous oxide). "I didn't feel it so much as the prick of a pin," he exclaimed. "A new era in tooth-pulling has arrived!"

Slave Labor Jobs

African-American slaves in the 19th century performed many of the jobs in the previous chapters, from laundress to skilled craftsman. Only a small minority, however, worked in mills, ironworks, and machine shops. The wealth of the Southern slave states came mainly from agriculture, not industry. In 1860, three-quarters of slave laborers worked on the land.

Field Slave

You work on a large cotton plantation. Your field gang plows the field, plants it, weeds the young plants with hoes, picks the cotton, and takes it to the cotton gin, where the seeds are separated from the lint.

August, September, and October are your least favorite months. This is cotton-picking time. You walk bent over in the heat, picking the fluffy cotton bolls from their prickly pods. You work from "can see to can't" in slave talk. When the moon is full, you sometimes work far into the night. Not all slave owners mistreat their slaves, but some do. If you don't pick fast enough, you may be whipped by the white overseer or his slave assistant, the "head driver."

At the beginning of the month, you receive just enough salt pork and cornmeal to last you for the month. You may be allowed to grow some vegetables in a small garden, but it is difficult to find time to tend your plot. If you are a woman, at the end of the day you must make dinner, clean your cabin, and take care of your children. You might have to do this alone if your husband has been sold to another plantation owner.

Revolts have been ruthlessly put down and escape is very difficult. Most runaways are eventually caught by slave patrols and returned to their owners. You do, however, fight back in the only ways that are available to you. You can pretend you are stupid, forcing overseers to repeat instructions or convincing them that you are unable to do certain jobs. You can pretend to be sick. Or you can steal food or break tools, gates, or carts and claim it was an accident.

SLAVE WORK SONG

Plantation slaves expressed their anger, despair, faith, and hope through song. Their powerful music laid the foundations for gospel, jazz, blues, rock, and rap. In this song, used by a field gang to set the pace of their work, "possum" refers to the overseer.

Caller: Now see that possum he works hard.

Chorus: Hoe Emma Hoe, you turn around dig a hole in the ground, Hoe Emma Hoe.

Caller: But he can't work as hard as me.

Chorus: Hoe Emma Hoe, you turn around dig a hole in the ground, Hoe Emma Hoe.

Caller: He sits a horse just as pretty as can be.

Chorus: Hoe Emma Hoe, you turn around dig a hole in the ground, Hoe Emma Hoe.

Caller: He can ride on and leave me be.

Chorus: Hoe Emma Hoe, you turn around dig a hole in the ground, Hoe Emma Hoe.

You can listen to this song on the Colonial Williamsburg website www.history.org by entering "Hoe Emma Hoe" on the site's search engine.

House Slave

Most slaves, if given the choice, would rather work in the "big house" than in the fields, but it's still no bed of roses. As a cook, for example, you work long hours in a hot little building behind the main house. You barely have the evening meal cooked over the fire in the old-fashioned fireplace before you have to grind the corn for the next day's bread or gather sticks for the morning fire. Nevertheless, you know that you and your children will never be hungry. In your kitchen, you also have more privacy and control over your workday than the other domestic servants. Maids, seamstresses, nurse-maids, butlers, and coachmen are under the constant supervision of the master and mistress.

SLAVE JOBS ON A LARGE PLANTATION

butler	plowman
cook	field hand
housemaid	wagon driver
nursemaid	cowman
seamstress	pigman
laundress	carpenter
gardener	mason
coachman	blacksmith
stable-hand	cooper
head driver	

CHAPTER 11

Change-the-World Jobs

These jobs change the way people think about something or the way they do something. Sometimes the people holding these jobs do change the world, but more often they just change a small part of it.

Social Reformer

You think about what isn't fair or doesn't work well in the world you live in and then try to do something about it. You need to be able to make a good argument for change, rally people to your cause, and never give up—reform can take time and courage. It doesn't pay well, or at all, so don't quit your day job.

You might choose to be an abolitionist and join the worldwide movement to end slavery. You could start an antislavery society or newspaper like William Lloyd Garrison did in the 1830s. You could stand up in public and speak out against slavery. Or you could help slaves escape to freedom as ex-slave Harriet Tubman did before the Civil War.

Do you think women should have the same rights as men? If you become a suffragist like Americans Elizabeth Cady Stanton and Susan B. Anthony and Canadian Nellie McClung, you fight for women's suffrage, the right of women to vote. It's a long fight. Canadian women will finally win the right to vote in 1918 and American women in 1920.

In the latter half of the century, social reformers fight for better treatment of prisoners, school reform, improved working conditions in factories, and children's rights. Fighting poverty leads to a new career: social worker.

Join us in our fight for liberty and equality.

"That man over there says that women need to be helped into carriages, and lifted over ditches, and to have the best place everywhere. Nobody helps *me* any best place. And ain't I a woman?"
— Freed slave Sojourner Truth, 1851 Women's Rights Convention, Akron, Ohio

Leader

Inventor

Do you have what it takes to lead people in the 1800s? Can you handle big ideas, such as building a railway across a continent? Can you unite people to fight against a common enemy, as Indian chiefs Tecumseh and Sitting Bull did in their efforts to hold on to their lands and way of life? Do you have the wisdom to lead your country through tough times—wars, epidemics, and thousands of people out of work? Can you give speeches that inspire people, as African-American leader Frederick Douglass did during the struggle to abolish slavery? Do you have an interesting pet? Just kidding—although John Quincy Adams, the sixth president of the United States, did have a pet alligator.

"What, to the American slave, is *your* Fourth of July? I answer: a day that reveals to him, more than all other days in the year, the gross injustice and cruelty to which he is the constant victim."

— Frederick Douglass, refusing to give a speech on the Fourth of July, 1852

You and your fellow inventors have been busy. You've imagined and produced an amazing number of new gadgets and machines. Some inventions change the world, while others, such as Nancy Johnson's 1843 ice-cream maker, just make life a little easier and more fun.

Your invention probably won't make you famous. The average person will look at it and say, "Wow, very impressive. What did you say it is?" Most people opening up a computer today and peeking inside wouldn't be able to name the parts or their inventors either. In the first half of the century, you're one of the many successful inventors who are manufacturers. You don't invent alone. You work with the machinists and other skilled workers in your machine shop to design, build, and improve steam engines, machines, or tools to make your business more successful.

You play an important role in the American Industrial Revolution. So what if no one knows your name? This is exciting work.

H.R. SMITH MACHINE CO. INC.

CHAPTER 12

Wartime Jobs

During the American Civil War of 1861 to 1865, some new inventions and ideas—hand-powered submarines, ironclad warships, and using hot-air balloons for spying on the enemy— didn't work. Other new technologies changed the way war was fought. The railway could move enormous numbers of soldiers and supplies to the battlefield, resulting in huge battles. The telegraph allowed field commanders to stay in close touch with each other. And the new cannons and long-range repeating rifles proved much more deadly than the old artillery and muskets.

Volunteer foot soldiers had read stories about earlier wars in magazines. They expected the fighting to be orderly, with lines of soldiers marching into battle. Instead, they found themselves in chaotic fighting, where the new weapons mowed down thousands of soldiers at a time, sometimes in a matter of minutes. Army commanders began building trenches and fortifications to protect their troops. Soldiers soon learned to stay low to the ground and to find cover.

More than 600,000 men, including 37,000 African Americans, died in the Civil War. Disease, rather than battle wounds, killed most of them. In the military camps, poor food, uncollected garbage, unburied sewage, and polluted water took a deadly toll.

Military Surgeon

You spend most of your time in what soldiers call the "butchering room" sawing off hands, feet, arms, and legs that are too mangled for repair. Before tackling each job, you wipe your bloody hands on an old rag. You give your patient ether or chloroform so that he doesn't feel the pain, then you remove the limb in minutes. After the operation, you wrap the stump in a recycled pus- and blood-stained bandage. You work hard and fast, not knowing that a little cleanliness would go a long way in helping your patients.

Doughboy

No, you don't bake cookies for the troops. More than three-quarters of the men in the Union and Confederate armies are foot soldiers, called "doughboys" after the lumpy brass buttons on their uniforms. The rest fight on horseback in the cavalry or serve as gunners in the artillery.

Like most excited young volunteers in 1861, you march off to war not really knowing much about being a soldier. Two out of ten soldiers are younger than 18, some as young as 11. At first, life in an army camp is fun. After chores, marching drills, and rifle practice, you spend the evening playing cards and checkers around the campfire.

Marching into battle is a different story. Your woolen uniform—gray if you're a Johnny Reb from the South and blue if you're a Billy Yank from the North—soaks up the heat in the summer and the cold rain in the winter. It crawls with lice and fleas. On the long marches to the battlefields, your feet become blistered and you're always hungry and thirsty. Small rations of rotten meat, moldy bread, wormy crackers, and bad coffee and water make you sick to your stomach and give you "the back-door trot."

After each battle, an officer reads the roll and you find out which of your friends have died. "I started in this thing a boy," one soldier wrote home. "I'm now a man."

"Then take your gun and go,
Yes, take your gun and go,
For Ruth can drive the oxen, John,
And I can use the hoe."
    — Civil War song

Nurse

As a paid or volunteer nurse in a hospital, you do what you can to help the sick and wounded. You wash, dress, and feed your patients and give them their medicine. If you work in a tent hospital set up near the battlefield, you might have to cook or wash clothes, find food on nearby farms, search the battlefield for wounded men, or drive a horse-drawn ambulance.

No trained nurses existed before the Civil War. After the Union won the war, nursing schools sprang up in several cities in recognition of the valuable work performed by wartime nurses.

"[I would] poke up the fire, add blankets, joke, coax and command, but continue to open doors and windows as if life depended on it … a more perfect pestilence box than this house I never saw—cold, damp, dirty, full of vile odors from wounds, kitchens, washrooms and stables."
— Louisa May Alcott, Union nurse and author of *Little Women*

Submarine Commander

You are the commander of the Confederate navy's latest secret weapon, the submarine torpedo boat.

The eight sailors under your command sit shoulder to shoulder. They drive the iron submarine through the water by turning a huge crank attached to a propeller. It's hard, sweaty work. You steer, work the dive fins, and keep the sub just under the waves: if your crew has to escape through the two hatches, you want the sub as close to the surface as possible.

Your mission is to sink a Union warship moored for the night. The submarine is armed with a harpoon-type torpedo full of explosives. Once you reach the ship, you ram the torpedo into its wooden hull. The crew quickly reverse the crank to pull the sub free, leaving the bomb behind. Then you set off the explosives by yanking a long rope stretching from the submarine to the torpedo. As the torpedo explodes, you and your crew try to get away. It's the last part that's tricky.

On February 17, 1864, the Confederate *H.L. Hunley* submarine sank the USS *Housatonic*. It was the first time a ship had been destroyed by a submarine. The *Hunley*'s crew never made it back to the surface.

Target, dead ahead! Take 'er down, men.

Spy

You believe strongly in your side's "cause" and are not afraid to take chances. If you are a woman, an ex-slave, or a newsboy, some people may not think you're smart enough to be a spy. This means you can watch the enemy with little fear of being caught. Union spies Elizabeth Bowser and William A. Jackson gathered information while working as servants in the Confederate president's house!

Spy catchers keep their eyes open for people who travel too much for no good reason. This is why you must pass your secret information to couriers rather than deliver it yourself. Couriers can slip through enemy lines without being noticed. Country doctors, for example, make excellent couriers because they can hide a message in their black bag and, if asked, say they are "out on a call."

Photographer

Famous New York photographer Mathew Brady has hired 20 cameramen to cover the war. You are one of them. However, you don't just sling a camera around your neck and bravely follow soldiers into battle. In fact, you never capture a battle scene; that's left to war artists.

Taking a photograph involves large cameras, tripods, fragile but heavy glass plates, bottles of chemicals, water, developing equipment, and a darkroom. You haul all of this around with you in a special horse-drawn wagon. It takes 20 minutes to make a single photograph. Even if you could shoot battle scenes, there would be nothing to see because the black powder used by the artillery covers the area with thick clouds of smoke. So, what do you shoot?

You photograph groups of soldiers (sometimes to help identify spies), prisoners of war, destroyed buildings, and battlefields after the fighting is over. You also take pictures of dead enemy soldiers to show people back home that the Union is winning the war. The printing technology of the time can't reproduce photographs in newspapers or illustrated magazines. Instead, thousands flock to public galleries to look at these grim images of war.

CHAPTER 13

Railroad Jobs

Even before the Civil War, the railroad had begun to take business away from steamboat, canal, stagecoach, and freighting companies. Trains could carry goods, mail, and people farther and faster than they had ever been carried before. Every other form of transportation seemed poky and old-fashioned in comparison.

Factory owners could now ship their products across the country rather than having to rely on local customers. More customers allowed them to expand their factories and experiment with new machines.

The railroad itself became the first "big business." It employed more people than any other industry—from engineers and conductors on the trains to blacksmiths, machinists, and carpenters in the repair shops to station agents and clerks in the depots. It also killed and injured hundreds of workers in spectacular train wrecks, boiler explosions, and other accidents. Life "on the line" was an exciting new way to make a living, but it was dangerous too.

Locomotive Engineer

You treat your steam locomotive as though it were your own personal racehorse. And in a way it is. You are the only one who can drive it. You are as proud of your new "iron horse" and what it can do as today's Formula One driver is of his new race car.

You make a good salary, about twice as much as a teamster, who drives a wagon full of goods. However, in the mid-1800s the number of days you work each month changes with the season. Because you are paid by the day—12 hours on weekdays and 10 hours on Saturdays—you are out of luck when snowstorms close down the track.

The engine's cab is your home away from home on the line. You share it with your fireman. Like the steamboat fireman, he keeps the fire burning in the boiler's firebox. If your locomotive is a "smoker," the two of you end the day covered with ashes.

Sitting proudly up in your engine, you look as though you're in charge of the train, but in fact you're not; the railroad conductor is. This well-dressed "dandy" collects the tickets, supervises the brakemen, and sometimes lords it over you. When this happens, you'd like to knock off his top hat. As it is, you ban him from the cab to keep him from spying on you and reporting back to a company manager.

Brakeman

The most dangerous part of your job is balancing on top of the two to five cars the conductor has assigned to you. When you hear the engineer blow the whistle signal for "down brakes," you run from car to car twisting each one's brake wheel. Like an automobile's brake pedal, the wheel operates the brakes, slowing down the train. As you brake each car, you scream as loud as you can, "All right here!" In bad weather and at night you can slip and fall or not see bridges in time to duck.

Coupling the cars injures more railwaymen than any other task. As the engineer slowly reverses, you guide the link of the last car in the train into the iron tube of the car to be linked up. Then you drop a pin through a hole just as the two pieces of the coupler are lined up. Sometimes the pieces don't fit together well and you crush a finger or two wrestling with the parts. At least you haven't fallen under the wheels yet. When applying for a new job, you just hold up your hands as proof of your experience.

At the turn of the century, a law is passed: all trains must be equipped with automatic air brakes and automatic couplers (invented in the 1870s). Unfortunately, it's too late for you.

"Orpheus Holmes, a very worthy man, who has been employed on the road as a brakeman since it was opened … was instantly killed by his head coming in contact with a bridge, while standing on top of a box car."
— First Annual Report of the Norfolk County Railroad, 1852

Construction Laborer

You are a laborer on one of the construction crews building the transcontinental railroad in the late 1860s. If you work for the Union Pacific pushing east from California, you are probably a Chinese immigrant. If you work for the Central Pacific heading west from Nebraska, you are likely an Irish immigrant or an ex-soldier.

Building the line is backbreaking labor done mostly by hand. Engineers and surveyors stake out the exact route. You cut down trees, blast through foothills with explosives, and dig tunnels through granite mountains so hard that it takes a day to drill eight inches (20 cm). Once the roadbed is level, you put down the tracks.

You work fast. The government has turned the building of the line into a race between the two railway companies. The one that builds the most track will make the most money. On the Plains, your crew can put down the wooden ties, lay the heavy iron rails on top, pound the spikes into the rails, and bolt on the connecting plates as quickly as a man can walk.

Bridge Engineer

Building a bridge is an engineering challenge. It can collapse under too much weight or be blown down if it isn't designed or built properly. As locomotives grow heavier and the boxcars carry more weight, your job is stressful in more ways than one. You don't really know how much stress your bridge can take until it's in use. The railway owners throw up bridges quickly and cheaply and avoid repairing them.

By the end of the century, your nightmares about trains plunging into rivers begin to disappear. You can design bridges of stronger materials, such as wrought iron and steel. A testing machine has been invented to measure how much stress a full-sized support can take. You can also give the builders "specifications," detailed instructions about the types of materials and construction methods to be used in building your bridge. All these improvements make train travel safer.

Waitress

Early train passengers traveling west had to put up with 20-minute stops at dirty shacks where the choice of food might be between a "chicken stew" of prairie dogs or a plate of canned beans. Fred Harvey changed all that. He opened restaurants at stops along the Santa Fe Railway serving decent food on sparkling china. In 1883 he began hiring young single women like you as waitresses.

Working in the Wild West sounds much more exciting than teaching or nursing at home in the East, so you sign a one-year contract to become a Harvey Girl. The restaurant staff include, from top to bottom, a manager, a chef, a head waitress, from 15 to 30 waitresses, a baker, a butcher, several assistant cooks, wash-up girls, a house-maid, and busboys. You can work your way up to become head waitress or even manager.

Rock-Hard Jobs

Rocks and ice played important roles in 19th-century America. People used blocks of ice and salt—the only rock we eat—to keep food from spoiling. In the country's ironworks, workers fired up the blast furnaces with coal and produced the iron needed for the railways' steam engines, tracks, and bridges. Quarry workers split off blocks of granite and sandstone for buildings, slate for fireproof roofing tiles, and marble for pillars and fireplace mantels. They also discovered the fossil footprints of dinosaurs in the brownstone blocks they sent to stonemasons in New York City.

Salt Maker

You own a saltworks. People call it a "lazy man's gold mine." You can make a lot of money without all the hard work required to mine gold. You put some big vats on the ocean beach, use a windmill to pump seawater into the vats, and let the sun evaporate the water, leaving the salt behind. At night and on rainy days, your workers close the sliding roofs over the vats.

If you own an inland saltworks, your salt comes from a briny spring. You boil the water in large kettles to produce the salt, or use evaporation vats. Tall watchtowers surround your many vats. When black clouds appear on the horizon, rain watchers in the towers ring a loud bell. Hundreds of workers and their families living in nearby villages race to the vats to roll down the covers. You give a small prize to the first family to close a complete row.

Coal Miner

When your 11-hour day begins, you walk, crawl or climb to your "chamber." It is one of many damp underground rooms in a room-and-pillar coal mine. The rooms line miles of underground passages and are divided from one another by pillars of coal and wooden timbers holding up the roof. Your flickering oil lamp is all that lights your way.

Your job is to dig large blocks out of the coal seam with a pick. You are paid by the ton. It helps to be short: seams are usually less than 6 feet (1.8 m) high and sometimes only 2 feet (0.6 m) high. If you're tall, you bend over or kneel to dig.

You're proud of the skills you learned from your father. No one tells you what to do in your chamber. The underground foreman only visits you once or twice a week. You and your young helper, often your son, load the blocks into a coal car and push it out into the main passageway. It is collected by a driver whose mules pull the cars along a track to the surface. If you need to go to the bathroom, you go over on the edge of the track. (It's polite to cover your "business" with dirt.)

As you dig, you listen for cracking sounds above your head. When a layer of shale begins to break, it makes a sound like thunder. The collapse of the roof or side walls is the number one killer in a mine, followed by fiery explosions and being crushed by the cars.

"My lamp is my sun, and all my days are nights."
— From a coal miners' song

DINNER WITH THE MINE RATS
Rats ate the mules' oats in the underground stables and drank the miners' lamp oil. Coal miners liked having them around, though. They believed they were safe from a cave-in as long as the rats scampered around their feet. When their furry friends left suddenly, the miners knew it was time to get out fast. The rats could probably detect changes in the size of their holes and hiding places as the rock layers shifted before the roof fell in. Some miners made pets of their "alarm" rodents, feeding them scraps from their dinner pails.

Ice Maker

You model yourself on the first "ice king," the very successful Frederic Tudor. In the early 1800s, he came up with the "crazy notion" that there was a market for ice in the tropics. He bought the rights to harvest ice on lakes near Boston, packed the blocks of ice in pine sawdust from New England's sawmills, and shipped them to the South, the West Indies, and even India. To increase the demand for his ice, he promoted ice cream, iced drinks, and iceboxes (old-time refrigerators).

Your enormous white-painted icehouse holds up to 50,000 tons of ice. When the lake beside the icehouse has frozen thick enough for men and horses to walk over it, you begin the harvest. After one horse-drawn plow scrapes off the snow, another one with huge teeth cuts the ice into 22- by-22-inch (56 x 56 cm) squares. Your workers use saws, chisels, and bars to remove the first blocks, leaving behind a wide channel of open water leading to the icehouse. The next squares they pry loose are floated along this channel.

You laugh at the idea of making artificial ice, but early in the next century refrigeration causes your business to melt away.

Breaker Boy

You work in a hard coal (anthracite) mine. This type of coal is broken up, washed, and cleaned in a building called a breaker. Your job is to pick pieces of slate out of the coal by hand.

This is a miserable, dirty job. You sit in a row beside other boys picking out pieces of rock as the coal tumbles along a chute. It's too noisy to talk to the boy beside you. You are hot in the summer and cold in the winter. You are learning nothing. By the end of the century, machines for cleaning coal begin to replace the thousands of 10- to 14-year-old boys working in the breakers.

WHEEZY WORK
Some workers coughed and wheezed a lot in this century. Rock and sand dust contain a crystal called silica, and large amounts of it can damage your lungs. Lung diseases affected coal miners, stone quarry workers, glassworkers, pottery workers, and workers in foundries (factories where melted metal was poured into sand molds to "cast" tools and machine parts).

Dinosaur Hunter

In the last quarter of the century, you're part of the dinosaur rush in the badlands of Wyoming. You work for scientist Othniel Charles Marsh, who is studying "the largest and most terrible animals that ever inhabited the earth." (This is how writers liked to describe dinosaurs, which weren't even called dinosaurs until 1841.)

Your job is to dig dinosaur bones out of the fossil quarry and ship them by train to your boss. How do you keep the brittle bones from breaking during the trip east? You wrap them in cloth dipped in plaster, just like the casts doctors have begun putting on broken bones.

Marsh is in a "bone war" with his rival Edward Drinker Cope. The two race to dig up bones, expand their collections, and publish the names, descriptions, and classifications of new dinosaurs. Both scientists make mistakes that future paleontologists will take years to unravel. Marsh names one dinosaur *Apatosaurus* and another one *Brontosaurus*, but they're actually the same species. To make matters worse, he puts the skull of another dinosaur, *Camarasaurus*, on his *Brontosaurus* skeleton. This isn't surprising: if a pile of never-seen-before bones were dumped in your room, would you know which bone went with what?

NATURALIST DROPS BOMBSHELL

Early geologists had noticed that older rock layers contained the fossils of simple sea creatures while the younger rock layers on top held the fossils of mammals. The fossil record seemed to indicate that the organisms that exist on earth change over time. In 1859, English naturalist Charles Darwin proposed that extinction was simply a part of nature. He suggested that the human species had evolved from earlier forms of life. His theory was hotly debated as people struggled with a different view of the origin of species than the Bible's story of God creating humans and animals in seven days.

CHAPTER 15

Great-Outdoors Jobs

Today the motto of Washington's National Museum of Natural History is "Understanding the natural world and our place in it." In the early 1800s, the attitude of most Americans towards the "great outdoors" was: "Let's eat it, hack our way through it, or just get rid of it, because, after all, there's more of it over the next hill."

By the end of the century, settlements stretched from ocean to ocean across what Americans had once called wilderness and Aboriginal peoples called home. People began to notice that the "noble primeval forest" was vanishing. (We can't be too smug about this, because forests and species today are still disappearing at an alarming rate.) John Muir and other early conservationists urged the government to set aside national forests and parks.

Workers in the crowded Eastern cities often envied those who worked outdoors without a clock in sight. They particularly liked to read about the cowboys of the "Wild West." In novels and boys' magazines, writers turned this low-paid ranch hand into a courageous hero. Just as an earlier generation had been drawn to the free-and-easy lifestyle of mountain men, young men looking for adventure left the cities to work as "cowpokes" on the open range.

Ranchwoman

As a rancher's wife or daughter, you are an excellent horsewoman. You may work outside on the ranch, roping and branding cattle with the men, or inside, doing household chores. You may do both.

If your husband or father dies, you have two choices: you can move into town or you can take over "the spread." Some women who become ranchers hire a foreman, while others manage the ranch themselves, earning the respect of their cowboys and the title "cattle queen."

Cowboy

Mexican vaqueros invented your job. They rode mustang horses, handled cattle from horseback, and wore "cowboy" hats and bandannas.

You are one of 10 to 15 cowboys on a long drive, herding funny-looking longhorn cattle from Texas to the railroad station in Dodge City or another cowtown. The trail boss has appointed you point rider in your outfit—the cowboy who rides at the head of the herd. You're thrilled because up until now you've been a drag rider at the rear of the 2,000 to 5,000 head of cattle, breathing thick dust all day, or a flank rider riding about two-thirds of the way back.

Your worst fear on the open range is a sudden stampede, particularly at night. Racing through the darkness while trying to slow down the thundering herd would test anyone's courage. You know cowboys who have been trampled to death or fallen from their horses. The leading cause of death for cowboys, though, is drowning during one of the many river crossings on a drive.

You don't like the "nesters" who have built fences around their farms, blocking the open range and trails. Sheepherders are just as bad. Range wars break out between cattlemen and farmers, but they end after the "great die-up" of 1886–87. Overgrazing on the grasslands and two brutally cold winters kill off cattle by the thousands and end the open range industry. Although you miss life on the trail, you still work as a cowboy. On the new fenced-in ranches, you drag cows out of mud, build fences, mend saddles and harnesses, fix windmills, and pile up hay for the winter.

Chuckwagon Cook

"Grub!" you shout, banging your pot lids together. Or, if you're feeling poetic, you might yell, "Ants in the butter, flies in the meat. If you cowboys are hungry, get up here and eat!"

You and your wagon of food travel with the cattle drives and serve up the four Bs—bread, beans, beef, and bacon. BURP! You cook your simple meals over a fire and the cowboys give them funny names:"son-of-a-gun stew" or "pigeons in disguise." Mostly you make sure that large pots of strong black coffee are always ready for the thirsty cowhands.

Lawman

You work in a dusty, smelly cowtown, where pigs roam about in the streets snacking on the garbage. When the cowboys reach your town after a long drive or come in from the ranch after payday, they often head for the saloons. There, they are joined by wagon teamsters and the soldiers from nearby forts. After drinking too much, they get into arguments with one another or with professional gamblers who cheat them out of their money. Fistfights, the drunken firing of six-shooters into the air, robberies, and horse thefts keep you busy "gathering in the sinners."

The law-abiding citizens of your town elect you to your low-paying job. Secretly they think you're a "necessary evil," a hired gunfighter who has more in common with the cowboys and gamblers you try to control than with church-goers like themselves.

BYE-BYE, BUFFALO

In 1869, a buffalo herd held up a train in Kansas for nine hours as it crossed the track. Just over a decade later, the Plains tribes' main source of food was nearly extinct. How did this happen?

To feed their track-laying crews, the railroad companies hired professional hunters to kill buffalo. The killing continued after Easterners began a fad: everyone wanted a buffalo lap robe to keep them warm in their carriages and sleighs. Then tanners discovered a way to turn buffalo hides into leather; hunters and their "skinners" sped up the slaughter. The Indians also tried to capture a share of the hide market, while amateur hunters killed the animals "for sport."

As more settlers moved into what had been set aside as Indian Territory, the government took over the best land for the settlers and forced the Indian nations onto reservations. A series of Indian Wars broke out as the Native people fought to preserve their way of life. By the 1880s, the buffalo were gone and Indians on reservations ate beef supplied by the government.

OUCH!

POW

BAM

Excuse me, could you fellows break it up now?

Lumberjack

In the fall and winter, you work in a Northern lumber camp. After chopping or sawing down trees all day, you eat and sleep in a log bunkhouse. It smells of drying socks and mittens, baked beans, and chewing tobacco. It smells of about a dozen stinky bodies too, since there is nowhere to take a bath. To go to the bathroom, you sit on a log in the woods with your bum hanging over the edge.

"Swampers" make trails and logging roads so that the logs you cut can be taken out of the woods. "Skidders" pull the logs along the trails with a team of horses and load them on sleighs at the logging road. If you're too young or too old to be a lumberjack, you can work as a "road monkey." You shovel frozen manure out of the sleigh ruts so that the sleighs loaded high with logs can run smoothly.

"The choppers and the sawyers,
They lay the timber low,
The swampers and the skidders,
They haul it to and fro."
— From "The Shantyboy's Song," *c.* 1840s

When the spring comes, you return to your family farm or work as a "river pig" on the logging drive. You help float the logs downriver to the sawmill. Jumping from log to log, you use your pike pole to push the logs apart so that they don't jam together. Unlike today, no one plants trees in the spring and summer to replace the ones you've cut down.

"One of the best ways to fool the lice was to turn your underwear inside out when you went to bed at night. The lice then spent most of the night finding their way from the outside to the inside and didn't have much time left to do any biting …"
— Lumberjack Walker D. Wyman, *c.* 1885

National Park Ranger

In 1886, the first park rangers in Yellowstone National Park—and later Yosemite, General Grant, and Sequoia national parks—were members of the United States Cavalry. They didn't become civilian employees of the federal government until 1916.

One of your jobs is to keep the animals in and the trappers and hunters out. By 1894, the buffalo in Yellowstone are the only ones living in the wild in the United States. They are in particular danger from poachers, because taxidermists will pay $500 for a buffalo head.

You ride through the park on boundary patrols. When you find someone trapping beaver or hunting buffalo, you throw him out of the park. In the winter, you do the same job on cross-country skis. It's dangerous fighting armed poachers who don't believe in game laws, not to mention bears that break into your patrol cabin once in a while to share your dinner. In the summer, you put out fires started by careless campers and arrest tourists for writing their names on rocks and geyser formations. You usually give the embarrassed graffiti artists a "tongue-lashing" before asking them to wash off their scribbles.

You think this is bad… you're also under arrest!

GRRRRRRR…..

OUTSIDE AND OUT OF WORK

Being a "tramp" is one outdoors "job" that no one wants. "Thousands of homeless men and women are to be seen nightly sleeping on the seats in our public parks, or walking the streets," reported a New York newspaper in 1874. Several major financial "panics" or "depressions" in the 19th century bankrupted businesses and threw thousands of people out of work. In small towns people could hunt or grow vegetables, but in the large cities they were forced to go "on the tramp." They traveled about the country looking for work.

"I have traversed seventeen states and obtained in that time six weeks' work," wrote one unemployed machinist in 1875. "I have faced starvation; been months at a time without a bed, when the thermometer was 30 degrees below zero. Last winter I slept in the woods … When I asked for something to keep body and soul together, I have been repulsed as a 'tramp and vagabond.'"

CHAPTER 16

Up-and-Down Jobs

These jobs are about moving people and information around. As the cities grew, more people lived in suburbs and were unable to walk to work. The cities began building street railway lines. Not everyone was happy about this new way to get around. Hackmen and deliverymen stuck behind the new horse-drawn streetcars yelled at their drivers. Passengers complained about the dirty cars. "Ladies and gentlemen are compelled to sit down on seats sticky with nastiness," wrote one critic.

One fan of the street railway was San Francisco businessman Andrew S. Hallidie. He sold the "wire rope" his father had invented to elevator manufacturers and mine owners. In 1869, Hallidie witnessed the type of horse-car accident that was common on his city's steep hills. An overloaded car was halfway up a hill when one of the horses pulling it slipped and fell. The driver tried to apply his handbrake, but the chain snapped and the car rolled backwards down the hill, dragging the horses with it.

If his cable could be used for elevators, Hallidie thought, why not streetcars, so that animals no longer had to pull them? By 1894, 5,000 horseless cable cars operated in the United States.

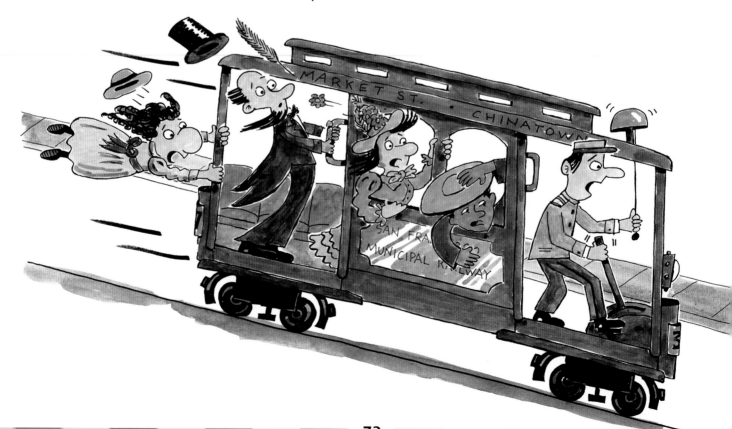

Cable-Car Gripman

Cable cars are pulled through the streets by a continuously running cable set between the tracks. Your job is to operate the car with a special handbrake that "grips" the cable to go and releases it to stop. A conductor collects the fares as you "drive."

You look out for boys on the road. They think it's fun to fish out the cable and attach boxes or toy wagons to it. People crossing the street are not amused.

Your worst fear, though, is a broken cable strand getting tangled up in your grip, preventing you from releasing the cable. When this happens, your car becomes a runaway. CLANG! CLANG! CLANG! You ring your bell, warning everyone in the path of the car. The conductor jumps off to alert the power house to stop the cable. Alarmed passengers leap to safety. To avoid a collision, the gripmen in front of you join the race, clanging their bells too in a wild dash through the streets.

Lineman

You're a 19th-century Spiderman working up among the webs of wires high above city streets or in the country along a line of wooden telegraph poles. This really is high-tech work. All the new technologies run along your wires— telegraph messages and, late in the century, electricity and telephone calls.

You wear spiked boots to climb the poles. When there are problems on the telegraph line, you head out to find the trouble spot. With your portable telegraph set, you can splice into the line and use Morse code (see page 83) to send messages to your supervisor. The worst part of the job is coating iron wires with smelly, sticky tar to prevent rusting.

By the end of the century, wiring contractors, the first electricians, are wiring homes and businesses for electricity and electric trolleys zip along the streets.

Sandhog

WARNING—This up-and-down job can twist you into a pretzel.

In the 1870s you work on the Brooklyn Bridge in New York City. The bridge will sit on two gigantic towers rising out of the water. Your job is digging two very deep holes for the towers.

To do this, you work inside a caisson, a watertight wooden structure that looks like an upside-down ship. (In fact, it was built in a shipyard and floated into position.) Although icy water sloshes at your feet, it doesn't rise any further because the caisson has been pumped full of enough compressed air to keep the East River out. You break up rock, which a dredging machine removes, and dig up sand and gravel, which pipes suck up to the surface. While you dig inside the hot caisson, masons build the granite-and-limestone towers above you. The stonework helps drive the caisson down to a depth of 78 feet (24 m) on the Manhattan side of the bridge.

At great depths underwater, the increased air pressure can cause head- and earaches. Frank Harris's landlady had a homemade remedy for the 15-year-old's earaches: "a roasted onion cut in two and clapped tight on each ear with a flannel bandage." Onions won't help, though, if you get the "bends." Like today's divers, sandhogs who come to the surface too soon without spending enough time decompressing suffer from tiny bubbles forming in their blood. Caisson disease can cause difficulty in breathing, dizziness, paralysis, and even death.

UP AND AROUND JUST FOR FUN

People had been riding merry-go-rounds, or carousels, since the previous century. Engineer George W. Ferris decided to turn the amusement ride on its end to celebrate the 400th anniversary of the discovery of America. The first Ferris wheel thrilled visitors to the 1893 World's Columbian Exposition in Chicago. No wonder—it was 250 feet (76 m) in diameter and each of its 36 glass-enclosed cars held 40 people.

Elevator Man

You repeat "What floor, sir?" or "What floor, ma'am?" over and over again, up and down, all day long. It's boring, but you're clean and dry, and you work in a modern department store, hotel, or office building. You control the speed of the elevator, bring it to a stop at each floor, and open and close the doors for your passengers.

From the day Elisha G. Otis showed his invention at the New York World's Fair in 1853, people have been nervous about elevator accidents. Some call elevators "man-traps." You assure new riders that a safety device keeps the elevator from falling if the cables break, then you pray that your boss has in fact installed a safe elevator rather than a cheap one.

"The stoppage of the elevator car brings a dizziness to the head and sometimes a nausea at the stomach. The internal organs seem to want to rise into the throat … If the body as a whole can be arrested at the same time with the feet, there will be no sickness. This can be done by placing the head and shoulders against the car frame."
— *Scientific American,* July 12, 1890

Fashion Jobs

The invention of the sewing machine in 1846 changed the fashion industry forever. One clothing factory hired 400 women to sew shirts on its new machines in place of the 2,000 seamstresses who had previously sewn them by hand at home. Men's shirts became the first "ready-made" clothing, followed by inexpensive pants, suits, and military uniforms. By 1850, New York City alone had over 4,000 work-shops employing 96,000 workers, two-thirds of them women.

Most women's clothing continued to be made as it had been in the past. Rich "society women" kept their dressmakers busy sewing separate outfits for breakfast, dinner, parties, church, committee meetings, and playing croquet in the garden. Other women sewed their own clothes and, if they could afford it, hired dressmakers to make them outfits for special occasions. By the 1860s, though, more and more women's clothing began to be made in the factory, including the sometimes deadly hoop skirt or crinoline. (Its birdcage-like frame made skirts look like upside-down teacups.) The invention of paper sewing patterns allowed home sewers to make better-fitting, more fashionable clothing, while the new mail-order catalogs gave rural women the opportunity to buy ready-to-wear clothes for themselves and their families.

Milliner

Betsy wants a new bonnet for spring. You show her different fabrics, artificial flowers, and ribbons as well as pictures of the latest styles in Madame Demorest's Quarterly Mirror of Fashions magazine. You aren't surprised when she says she absolutely must have egret feathers. You've put whole birds on wealthier customers' hats.

As a milliner, you make custom hats to order. Your work is creative, pays fairly well, and, if you own your own shop, allows you to be independent. Every town has a milliner because no decent woman goes out in public during the day without first putting on a hat.

Department Store Owner

You are very proud of your new six-story dry goods store with its modern plate-glass windows, elevators, and electric lighting. It covers an entire city block. The narrow, shelf-lined stores of your competitors look small and dingy in comparison.

Male ushers (today's greeters) say hello to your customers at the door and show them the way to the right department—carpets, ribbons, dresses, hats, stockings, gloves, blankets, even mattresses. You hire male department heads and sales clerks as well as young "cash boys" to take the customers' money to the cashier's cage for change. At the end of the century, you also hire women sales clerks and "cash girls." They do the same job as the men and boys but for a lower salary.

You do have one woman supervisor on staff. She bosses around the hundreds of women sewing-machine operators in the top-floor work-rooms. They make many of the items sold on the lower floors. Outworkers do any special work that is required. You pay a home seamstress $3.75 for seven days' work putting fancy stitching on a dress, pay $20 for the cloth, and sell the dress for $85 in the store. No wonder you're a rich man!

"About 11 o'clock on Thursday night a shocking accident occurred, resulting in the death of Miss Kate Degraw … as the deceased was being assisted from the carriage, the horses took sudden fright and dashed off at furious speed. The young lady's crinoline became entangled in the steps of the carriage, and with her head and shoulders dragging upon the ground, the horses made the circuit of the village twice before the citizens could stop them."
— *New York Times,* June 17, 1865

"I don't get the salary the men clerks do, although this day I am six hundred sales ahead! Call this justice? But I have to grin and bear it, because I am so unfortunate as to be a woman."
— Iowa shoe saleswoman, 1886

77

Sweatshop Worker

You are a young immigrant who has found work as a sewing-machine operator in a sweatshop. Your boss runs a contract shop in his run-down apartment. He competes with other contractors for work from clothing manufacturers, who supply him with cut pieces to sew together. The difference between the money he receives for the contract and the money he pays workers like you is his profit. He increases his profit by "sweating" his workers: you are made to work long hours for low pay under unhealthy conditions.

It's not a fun job. You work from five in the morning until nine at night in a dirty, badly lit, often windowless, and sometimes locked room. The machines run by foot power. The faster you sew, the more money you make, since you are paid by the piece. Exhaustion, malnutrition, and disease claim the lives of many of your fellow workers, including the young men who are hired as pressers.

Ragpicker

You share a damp basement room in New York City with 10 other immigrants. Your own clothes are rags, but that's not why you're called a rag-picker. Every day, you walk down to the river to search the garbage barges for old pieces of cloth. You paw through the stinky piles before the flat-bottomed boats are towed out to sea and the garbage dumped.

Most ordinary people in the 1800s are recyclers. Women collect rags to make into quilts for beds or hooked rugs for doormats. The faded, dirty bits that are thrown away are of no use to anyone but you. You take them to a rag dealer, who sells them to a paper mill. Until paper began to be made from wood pulp in the mid-1800s, it was all made from linen and cotton. Today's paper money still is.

CHAPTER 18

Working-for-the-City Jobs

By the late 19th century, cities were bursting at the seams. People from other lands had flooded in, looking for a better way of life. Some found it while others lived in poverty. African Americans, Mexicans, and Asians, in particular, often had trouble finding well-paying jobs because of the prejudices of native-born white Americans.

The cities were run by politicians whose chief aim was to keep themselves in power. They often bought the votes of immigrants by giving out jobs and gifts—a basket of food or a bag of coal. To pay for the gifts and make money for themselves, corrupt politicians asked for extra money, or kickbacks, from businesses doing work for the city, sometimes with disastrous results.

In 1875, New York firefighters were demonstrating the newly invented aerial ladder. They were 98 feet (30 m) in the air when, much to the horror of the crowd watching, the ladder began swaying. It soon snapped in half, killing three of the men. Scandal broke out when it was discovered that the chief of the board of fire commissioners had demanded a kickback on the sale of the ladders to the city. The manufacturers had made the ladders of bad wood in order to pay the commissioner and still make a profit.

Amazingly, corrupt politicians did manage to tackle some of the biggest problems cities faced at that time: fire, crime, disease, and pollution. They set up professional fire and police departments. They hired engineers to improve water-supply and sewage-disposal systems to help prevent epidemics. (By 1880, nearly one-third of city families had installed indoor toilets and bathtubs.) They hired garbagemen and street sweepers to rid the streets of disease-carrying garbage and manure, which free-roaming pigs used to devour as late as the 1850s in some cities. Finally, they hired landscape architects to design parks. In the stinky cities, people badly needed a place to go where they could take a breath of fresh air (although the rich came mainly to show off their new carriages and clothes).

Firefighter

Volunteer companies fought fires up until the mid-1860s in some cities. They continue to do so in some rural areas even today. Although "fire laddies" often worked hard and bravely, they sometimes seemed more interested in fighting one another than fighting fires. The first company to reach a fire and hook up its hoses to the water supply won glory and sometimes money from the property owner's insurance company. More and more people demanded professional firefighting crews after watching buildings burn while volunteers fought in the streets over whose company had reached the fire first.

You are a paid professional firefighter working with the latest technology. Instead of relying on people ringing bells to tell you where a fire has broken out, telegraph alarm boxes set up through-out the city pinpoint the blaze. Your depart-ment's steam fire engine needs fewer men to operate it than the old hand-pumped engines.

A new hook-and-ladder rig with a "big stick," an 85-foot (26 m) aerial ladder, reaches people on upper floors that ordinary ladders can't reach. If the big stick isn't long enough, you use a scaling ladder, a single rod with crossbars and a hook at the end. This is tricky. You lift the ladder up to the window of the floor above you, hook it over the sill, and climb up. Once you reach that window, you break it, climb through, drag up the ladder, and continue up.

Police Officer

HALT in the name of the law!

You're the 1890s version of a traffic cop. You chase down speeding horse-drawn carriages and rein in runaway horses on the latest police equipment—a bicycle. Obviously you have to be a very good cyclist. One of New York City's "Scorcher Squad" caught up to a carriage racing away from a crime scene, leapt off his bike into the carriage, and arrested the surprised driver.

As a "copper" (you wear a copper badge on your blue uniform), you have other duties besides arresting criminals. You might shoot stray dogs, inspect tenement houses, license steam boilers, take care of lost children, or provide shelter for homeless people in the cellar of your police station. You enforce city bylaws against kite flying or ball playing in the streets, especially on Sundays. In New York City you even clean the streets until a street cleaning department takes over in 1881.

POOP AND SCOOP JOBS

Street Sweeper: Horse owners did not practice "poop and scoop"; the city paid street sweepers to do it. Each horse in a city deposited 15 to 30 pounds (7 to 14 kg) of manure on the streets every day. In the late 1800s, about 3.5 million horses trotted around American cities. That was a lot of poop to clean up and cart away to a manure pit.

Housewife: If a woman didn't have indoor plumbing or domestic servants, she emptied and cleaned her family's chamber pots every morning. These pots looked like large china cups. They were kept under beds and used as toilets at night or upon waking to save a trip to the outdoor privy.

Nightman: Landlords and house owners paid these men to empty privies. They were allowed to work only from 10 p.m. until 3 a.m., which is why they were called nightmen. No one wanted to run into these people and their loads.

WHAT'S THAT SMELL?

Engineers who built sewers had to convince city residents that sewer gas wouldn't kill them. No one really knew what this was— probably just a very bad smell—but it was the latest thing to worry about in the 1870s and '80s. According to the author of *Sewer Gas and Its Dangers*, it floated out of sewer pipes and robbed "men of ambition and women of beauty" or, worse, killed them in their beds. By the end of the century, people understood that microorganisms, or bacteria, caused diseases, not sewer gas.

CHAPTER 19

Entertaining Jobs

Couch potatoes didn't exist in this era. The only screen to watch at home was the fire screen starring the Dancing Flames. Americans devoured newspapers, novels, and magazines. Would-be frontier farmers and their wives read guidebooks while would-be socialites read etiquette books. And would-be millionaires? They read rags-to-riches stories. After all, if Scottish immigrant Andrew Carnegie could begin his career as a 13-year-old bobbin boy in a textile mill and rise to become the richest steel baron in the world, why couldn't they?

People could only read so many books and magazines, play so many games, and sing together around the piano so many times, though, before they had to get out of the house to have some fun. They flocked to amusement parks, soda fountains, dance halls, theaters, early movies, and concert halls. If you didn't live in a city, the world of entertainment came to your nearest town. Actors, singers, musicians, and circus performers went "on the road," just as they do today.

By the end of the century, baseball was quickly becoming the "national pastime." College football, basketball, and boxing had their fans too. Croquet and bicycling appealed to both men and women. To ride their new bikes, women could finally put on some comfortable clothes—puffy pants called bloomers.

Telegraph Operator

Newspaper reporters mainly wrote about local news early in the century. When the New York *Evening Post* appeared in 1801, a front-page story covered the problem of pigs taking over the city streets. But after telegraph lines began crisscrossing the country and a transatlantic cable was laid in 1866, newspapers became the Internet of their time. Although the papers didn't report national and international news instantly, even yesterday's news amazed readers.

You're a human computer in the Associated Press telegraph office. While a computer uses two digits (0 and 1) to send and receive messages, you use a dot and a dash (dot-dash for A, dash-dot-dot-dot for B, and so on) to tap out messages on your instrument's key. Receiving messages by listening to the clicks on a Morse sounder is automatic for you now, like understanding a foreign language. One telegrapher becomes such an expert at receiving Morse code that he can copy a message in French and English at the same time, writing with both hands. Sending telegrams is considered more difficult, mentally and physically, than receiving them. (Like today's computer operators, you can develop severe muscle pain in your sending arm.)

You like going to baseball games with a reporter. As the game is played, he dictates his story to you and you send it to the pressroom.

"All work and no play make Jack a dull boy."
— Popular saying

Newspaper Publisher

Your job is to sell as many copies of your newspaper as possible. The first step is to ask your headline writers to come up with shocking headlines for news stories: "Human Monsters Who Rob Corpses," "Screaming for Mercy," that kind of thing. Newsboys shout out the headlines on street corners.

Promotional stunts that will draw attention to the paper work well. You wish you had thought of New York publisher Joseph Pulitzer's idea of sending a woman reporter around the world. Nellie Bly (her real name was Elizabeth Cochran) raced against the fictional Phileas Fogg in Jules Verne's popular novel *Around the World in Eighty Days*. She made it in 72 days and sold thousands of papers as readers followed her adventures. Adding a comic page to your Sunday edition can't hurt. As more people read your paper, more businesses will want to advertise in it.

Dime Novel Writer

Hmmm, let's see... should our villain shoot him between the eyes now or leave him in the desert to rot later?

BEST-SELLING BROWNIES

Palmer Cox was the J.K. Rowling of his time. This Canadian-born illustrator and poet published 16 best-selling children's books about brownies—not the kind you eat. Here's how he described them: "These brownies, like fairies and goblins, are imaginary little spirits, who are supposed to delight in harmless pranks and helpful deeds. They work and sport while weary households sleep, and never allow themselves to be seen by mortal eyes." Cox's brownies conquered North America after *The Brownies' Ride* appeared in 1883. They appeared on china plates, in games and puzzles, as well as in ads to sell products. They were still so popular in 1900 that George Eastman, the inventor of the first handheld camera, called his new pocket-sized camera the Brownie.

Thousands of young working-class people pay a nickel or dime to buy one of your novels in the 1800s. But unlike Mark Twain, Charles Dickens, or Louisa May Alcott, your work is unknown today. In fact, your name rarely appears on any of your books.

You write dime novels. A publisher hires you to write cowboy tales, detective stories, working-man novels, or tearjerkers (heartbreaking romances with dying heroes or heroines and lots of exclamation points). You must have a good imagination and be able to write 30,000 words—the length of most cheap novels—very quickly. When you aren't writing a dime novel, you support yourself by teaching or writing newspaper articles, plays, or local histories.

TWO MUST-READS

Women wrote two of the century's most influential books. In 1852, Harriet Beecher Stowe's best-selling novel *Uncle Tom's Cabin* persuaded many people to support the ending of slavery. During the Civil War, Abraham Lincoln is reported to have said to Stowe, "So you are the little lady that has brought this big war." Helen Hunt Jackson wrote about the mistreatment of Native Americans in her 1881 non-fiction book *A Century of Dishonor*.

Soda Fountain Owner

You own a drugstore and have put in a soda fountain to cash in on the latest fad. This machine makes soda water and keeps it cool with blocks of ice. You mix the plain soda water with flavored syrups to make delicious five-cent drinks. In the days before air conditioning or even electric fans, young people like to meet their friends at your counter to cool off with one of your bubbly drinks.

You also make ice-cream sodas, which should really be called ice *and* cream sodas because they're made with slivers of ice, sweet cream, syrup, and soda water, not ice cream. You hire a soda clerk to take on the time-consuming job of shaving the ice. Wearing a special glove, he scrapes a small block of ice across the blades of a planer. It's like grating cheese, only trickier.

Professional Baseball Player

Playing baseball for eight months each year earns you as much money as a skilled craftsman makes in a year. However, you give up your independence for a good wage.

In the early 1880s, you sign a contract that prevents you from playing for another club unless you are traded or your contract is sold. The club manager runs your life on and off the baseball diamond. He can fine or suspend you for breaking the rules. One owner even hires private detectives to check up on his players to see if they are honoring their pledge not to drink alcohol.

The game's rules change every year. Unlike today, for example, you can throw a spitball but not a curveball. Some players bend the rules or "play dirty." They hide extra balls in the tall outfield grass and trip base runners. One player encourages his team's fans to flash small mirrors, blinding the other team's fielders as they try to catch fly balls. Now that's foul ball!

Wild West Show Performer

William F. Cody, known as "Buffalo Bill," had worked as a Pony Express rider and a hunter supplying buffalo meat to railroad workers in the late 1860s. After writing about his frontier adventures in novels and plays, he staged a new form of live outdoor entertainment, the wildly popular Wild West Show. Talented performers showed off their fancy riding, roping, and shooting skills and acted out thrilling frontier scenes— a pretend "Grand Hunt" with real buffalo, elk, and mountain sheep, Pony Express riders racing across the Plains to deliver the mail, and a pretend Indian attack (by real Indians) on a wagon train and a stagecoach.

In the 1880s, you tour with the show as one of its many Native performers. Your job is controversial. Some people believe the show gives a false picture of Native Americans as "savages" rather than as the victims of westward expansion. Others think that allowing you to keep your long hair and Native dress lets you be yourself in a way that is impossible on the reservations. Certainly, you can earn more money as a performer than as a farmer trying to raise crops on poor land. It's more fun, too.

"Backstage" behind the arena, you talk to audience members whose tickets allow them to wander around the grounds. They particularly like to look at the fine horses you ride. (People admired superb horses then the way we admire sports cars today.) They also want to catch a glimpse of the show's stars, particularly sharpshooter Annie Oakley, who can shoot a cigarette out of a man's mouth.

Mistress: Maggie, have you put fresh water in the goldfish bowl?
Maid: No, they ain't drunk up what I gave 'em yesterday.
— Comedian's joke, 1890s

"He'd fly thro' the air with the greatest of ease,
A daring young man on the flying Trapeze;
His movements were graceful, all girls he could please
And my love he purloin'd [stole] away."
— From the song "The Flying Trapeze" by George Leybourne, 1868

Snake Charmer

In what other career would your job title be "The Queen Supreme of the Serpent Kingdom, Absolute Mistress of the Writhing, Strangling Monsters"? You work in a sideshow tent rather than under the "big top," the huge tent where the trapeze artists, clowns, animal trainers, and bareback riders perform. The public walk by and stare at you and the other strange sideshow acts—the Elastic Skin Man, the Tattooed Lady, the Lady Giantess, the Smallest Man on Earth.

Unlike the act of famous escape artist Harry Houdini, who began his career in the circus, your act doesn't take much skill. You hang a boa constrictor or two around your neck and use your "supernatural powers" to "charm" them. Actually, you control them with a sponge soaked with ether tucked away in your corset. If the snakes start to tighten their coils, you knock them out with the ether when no one is looking.

Easy there, sweetie. I'm already wearing a corset!

Actor

You are the lead actor in a resident stock company, a group of actors who perform plays in one particular theater for a season. As well as taking the leading tragic and comic roles, you may serve as the company manager, stage manager, and sometimes even scene painter. There is no director.

The wealthy members of your audience sit in the boxes near the stage, the middle class in the orchestra seats, and the poor in the balconies. The stage itself is usually dimly lit, with very little scenery. To make yourself seen and heard, you must use big, sweeping arm movements and speak your lines clearly. With passion! With the correct pronunciation! With poetic rhythm! (Shakespeare wrote most of the plays your company performs, so this last tip is important.)

Women act in the same classic style as men or in the "emotional" style. Are you good at crying, screaming, and throwing yourself into chairs in deep despair? If so, you might want to audition for the "lady in distress" role in a weepy melodrama, this century's soap opera.

Big-Business Jobs

The years at the end of the century are called the Gilded Age. *Gilded* means "covered with gold," and the big business owners of the time were certainly golden. They had a knack, not for blowing glass or rolling dough, but for making money—and lots of it.

Wealthy railroad men rode through their own lands, some as large as small European countries, in fancy private railway cars. One of them, Cornelius Vanderbilt, left his son a fortune of $100 million when he died in 1877. Americans who made an average wage of $350 a year at that time found this sum astounding. There had always been rich Americans, but not *that* rich.

Vanderbilt and his fellow big business owners became known as the Robber Barons. Some people wondered if a civil war that had destroyed one ruling class, the Southern slaveholders, had produced another, the Northern industrialists.

Robber Baron

How can you be a thief and a lord at the same time? Easy. According to your critics, you steal from your workers and turn yourself into a very rich industrial prince.

Your job is to run a giant corporation. Like other industrialists, your favorite word is *control*. You want to control your workers, control the politicians who make laws that affect your business, and control the markets in which you sell your products. To do this, you find ways to cut wages and other costs, give money to friendly politicians, and drive as many of your competitors out of business as possible, thus creating a monopoly. If you've ever won a game of Monopoly, you know the power a steel, petroleum, coal, cattle, lumber, or railroad baron feels.

Some "captains of industry" build libraries and donate thousands of dollars to charities. Others spend, spend, spend.

Socialite

Your name appears in the city's Social Register, a listing of the most important people in "high society." You spend your time organizing your household staff, holding parties, planning holidays, shopping, visiting friends, and raising money for charity.

Here are a few tips on how to show off your wealth, which some people think is a large part of a snob's job. First, hire as many servants as you can: a nurse for the children, a cook, an upstairs and a downstairs maid, a waitress or butler, and a coachman are the bare minimum. Second, display as much stuff made of silver as possible, from forks and knives to picture frames on the grand piano. Old Indian ceremonial baskets are the latest collectible and look "heavenly" in your cluttered parlor. (Ignore the fact that the government doesn't allow Native Americans to hold their sacred ceremonies anymore.) Third, throw a huge party and decorate your indoor pool with men swimming around dressed up as goldfish (real goldfish are *so* middle class). Finally, travel to Europe each summer with at least 30 trunks and suitcases. (Any fewer would make you look positively poor, dear.)

THE FEATHERED HAT THAT KILLED MILLIONS

In the last quarter of the century, professional hunters killed millions of wild birds and sold their feathers to hatmakers. In the Florida Everglades, they slaughtered adult egrets at their nesting sites, leaving the young to die of starvation. Boston socialites Harriet Hemenway and Minna Hall founded the Massachusetts Audubon Society in 1896 after reading about these atrocities. They convinced prominent women like themselves to stop wearing feathered hats and to work with their new group to protect birds. Within six years of the founding of their group, Audubon societies were formed in 26 other states and bird-watching became a popular pastime.

Other socialites formed the National Consumers' League in 1899 to help the poorly paid sweatshop workers who made ready-made hats and clothing. Through their power as consumers, they hoped to change the working conditions of the people who made the clothing and other items they bought.

My dear, may I have a word with you about that hat you're wearing?

Architect

You design all kinds of buildings, from private homes to office towers. Before you draw up a plan that builders can follow, you need to find out how your client will use his new building. A robber baron who likes to dance and collect the latest technological toys, for example, will need a mansion with a ballroom, a garage for his new automobile, and pipes and wires for all the latest inventions: electric lights, steam heating, elevators, and telephones. As well as making sure the building will work well for your client, you also imagine how you want it to look inside and out. You are an artist as well as an engineer.

The "Great Fires" of Chicago in 1871 and Boston in 1872 keep you very busy. Your modern high-rise buildings rise out of the rubble of these cities' downtowns. The invention of the elevator and new construction methods using cast iron and steel beams have made it possible for you to design buildings taller than the old four or five stories. By the end of the century, you are designing steel-framed "skyscrapers" that soar 30 stories into the air. Your plans set in motion an army of construction workers, from foremen, carpenters, masons, bricklayers, painters, and plasterers to unskilled laborers.

ON STRIKE

Up in their skyscrapers and behind the walls of their estates, the Robber Barons sometimes seemed indifferent to the hardships and suffering of their workers. Factories had become large, dirty, noisy, and often dangerous places to work. In the hot steel mills, for example, the men worked long shifts without a meal break every day except Christmas and the Fourth of July. One "slip" meant disaster when you worked around molten metal, blast furnaces, and heavy equipment. "It's like any severe labor," said one steelworker. "It drags you down mentally and morally just as it does physically. Twelve hours is too long."

Men and women formed labor unions and went on strike over long hours, dangerous working conditions, and low wages. They won some victories late in the century—an eight-hour day for government employees and state laws governing hours of work and safety standards. But like child labor laws, many of these laws were not enforced, and workers would have to wait until the next century for their rights to be acknowledged and protected.

Stenographer-Typist

You are a woman in a man's world. Many of your co-workers are men because clerical work is still considered "men's work."

You have two special skills: shorthand writing and typing. Shorthand is like early text messaging. It drops the vowels and uses symbols to take the place of common words (for example, a period for "the" and a short slash for "and"). Your boss dictates letters to you, which you write down in shorthand as he speaks. Stenographers used to write these letters out neatly in longhand, but you use a typewriter.

Women were chosen to demonstrate the new typewriters because better-educated women often knew how to play the piano; it was thought that this skill would make them natural typists. Unlike today's computer keyboard, you have to pound the keys to make each letter's type bar hit the paper. Whoops! Did you make a mistake? You can't hit the "delete" key because there isn't one. You'll have to rub out your mistake with a typewriter eraser and hope your boss doesn't notice.

Office Clerk

The number of "blue-collar" workers—manual laborers who wear work clothes—doubles between 1860 and 1880. For the first time, more people rely on wages than are self-employed. You're a wage earner too, but you're a "white-collar" worker. You wear a white shirt and do clerical work in a bank, stock brokerage, life insurance company, government department, or corporate head office.

Unlike early-19th-century merchants, who ran successful import-export businesses with the help of a few clerks, big business owners have large office staffs to keep track of their far-flung empires. They need bookkeepers, clerks, copyists, and office boys. Except in banks and insurance companies, the office staff connect the "brains" of a company—its managers—with the "hands"— production workers.

You think of your job as the first rung on "the ladder of success," a way to learn the ins and outs of a business before advancing to a management position or opening your own small business. But as companies become larger, gobbling up the smaller companies, it becomes ever more difficult for clerks like you to open their own successful businesses.

Telephone Operator

You are excited to be one of the first telephone operators, a new career for women. On your head you wear a metal-and-rubber headset that connects you to the switchboard in front of you. Your job is to connect and disconnect callers with cords and plugs. You must have a nice speaking voice and be "ladylike" talking to customers—no rude sighs or hanging up. Callers ask all sorts of questions, the most common one being, "What time is it, please?"

You could be promoted after many years to chief operator or office manager. However, because this is "women's work," your salary is kept low. The company assumes that you live with your parents and will leave as soon as you find a husband, so you don't qualify for a "family wage" as men do.

In 1876, only 3,000 telephones exist in the United States. By 1900, there are 1.4 million. Now that's a big business!

ON VACATION

In the 1840s, doctors began recommending travel in the countryside to cure "wear-and-tear" sickness. At high risk were businessmen who strained their brains and upset their tummies working in the city. Summer resorts offered a cure in the form of boating, bowling, swimming, riding, fishing, and hunting.

After the Civil War, white-collar workers began taking a summer vacation too. Businessmen paid attention to the medical warnings about overwork and gave their "brain workers" one week's paid vacation each year. Working for the government must have been particularly stressful, because federal clerks enjoyed a rare one-month holiday.

"In the gray of the morning they [cable cars] come out of the up-town, bearing janitors, porters, all that class which carries the keys to set alive the great downtown. Later, they shower clerks. Later still, they shower more clerks."

— Author Stephen Crane, late 1890s

Recommended Further Reading

Many wonderful books have been written about the 19th century. It's always fun to read books set in that period by authors of the time, although they are not always easy to read and you may have to wait until you are older to enjoy them. Authors to explore include: Louisa May Alcott, L.M. Montgomery, James Fenimore Cooper, Mark Twain, Laura Ingalls Wilder, Robert Louis Stevenson, Charles Dickens, and Lewis Carroll. Your teacher or local librarian will be able to suggest titles for you to try.

Here are some suggestions for fiction and non-fiction books about the 1800s written by a few of today's authors:

Bolden, Tonya. *Maritcha: A Nineteenth-Century American Girl* (2005).
This book, which is illustrated with old photographs, maps, and illustrations, is based on the unpublished memoirs of a girl who lived in mid-century New York City.

Delano, Marfé Ferguson. *Inventing the Future* (2002).
An illustrated book about tireless inventor Thomas Alva Edison and his many inventions.

McCaughrean, Geraldine. *Stop the Train* (2001).
In this prize-winning novel, a family starts a new life on the prairies of Oklahoma in the late 1800s but find themselves joining their neighbors in a battle with the railroad company to save their town.

Peck, Richard. *The River Between Us* (2003).
A Civil War novel about Tilly Pruitt, her family and two mysterious strangers who arrive one day on the steamboat from New Orleans.

Swanson, Wayne. *Why the West Was Wild* (2004).
A non-fiction book about the cowboys, settlers, lawmakers, and outlaws of the Wild West illustrated with photographs, posters and reproductions of paintings by famous 19th-century artists.

ACKNOWLEDGMENTS
People spend their entire lives researching just one event that happened in the 1800s, so writing a book that spans the century and many different subjects was challenging. I owe a debt of gratitude to Priscilla Galloway, the author of the marvelous *Archers, Alchemists, and 98 Other Medieval Jobs You Might Have Loved or Loathed*, the predecessor to this book. She covered a thousand years, not a mere hundred. Her observation that a book for young readers inevitably simplifies and condenses what is known and presents material that experts don't always agree upon, helped me keep things in perspective during my own research and writing. In the end, I chose to include stories and historical nuggets that I thought readers might find as fascinating, unexpected, sad or funny as I did.

Working on this book has been a wonderfully creative process. I would like to thank editor Laura Scandiffio, copy editor John Sweet, creative director Sheryl Shapiro and illustrator Martha Newbigging, whose amazing illustrations form the heart of this book. A special thank you to Dr. Joshua B. Freeman for his expert advice. I would also like to thank my family and friends for their encouragement, particularly my husband, Erich.

Index